Advance praise for *Come to Believe* . . .

"Stephen Katsouros has created one of the most important experiments in educational equity underway in the United States today."

—Paul Tough, author,
Helping Children Succeed: What Works and Why

"I strongly believe in the power of a Jesuit education. Both of my children and my five grandchildren have been educated at Jesuit schools. When Fr. Katsouros shared with me his vision for Arrupe College—the first-ever Jesuit community college in the United States—I immediately wanted to be a part of it. One of my priorities in life is to help provide the opportunity of higher education to inner-city young men and women. Many of these students are immigrants like me, and by helping to provide a Jesuit education for them, the future of America can be strengthened. Fr. Katsouros's account of the first year in the life of the new Arrupe College captures the faith, hope, and love required to make a school like this work. This book is a testimony to the Jesuits and gives us all hope that more young people will have access to higher education on the journey to becoming their best selves."

—Lidia Bastianich,
best-selling author and restaurateur

"Arrupe College is the best idea the American Jesuits have had in the last 25 years. And the story of how the nation's first Jesuit community college got off the ground is one of the most compelling stories you'll read this year. With his years of background in education and working with those on the margins, Father Katsouros introduces you to some of the most inspiring young men and women you could ever hope to meet."

—James Martin, SJ, author, *Jesus: A Pilgrimage*

"This story of the amazing students of Arrupe College proves that Pedro Arrupe's wisdom still shapes and influences a new generation. These kids truly are being formed into 'persons for others.' In opening their doors to students who might not have otherwise been able to attend university, Arrupe is making a priceless investment in the future. Chicago and the world need Arrupe College."

—Susana Mendoza, Illinois State Comptroller

W9-CJS-888

"Pope Francis often reminds us that we must go to the periphery of society to meet and help those in need, to accompany them and to learn from them as well. Arrupe College is an extraordinary model of the compassion that Francis challenges us to live daily. *Come to Believe* is the exciting story of this unique school's first year—the remarkable students and the dedicated staff and volunteers jump off the page and into your heart. And you will never be the same. This is an inspiring and hopeful read—I highly recommend it!"

—Mark K. Shriver, author,
Pilgrimage: My Search for the Real Pope Francis
and president of Save the Children Action Network

"I am a firm believer in the power of Jesuit education to open doors for young women and men, especially those on the margins and in the greatest need. My undergraduate education at Marquette University empowered me to embrace God's dream for me rather than abide by false limitations of others. Arrupe College is empowering its students—primarily Latino and African-American—in much the same way. Our city, and so many cities across the country, needs Arrupe College. It's the perfect complement to traditional Jesuit schools, as well as Nativity-model and Cristo Rey model schools—all of which are game changers in their own right."

—Cherryl T. Thomas,
President and CEO of Ardmore Associates;
deputy chief of staff, Chicago Mayor Richard M. Daley

"This important book tells a story that's unusual—and perhaps it shouldn't be. Chicago's Loyola University, challenged to think about the education of lower-income students, actually started a new two-year college with a mission to admit poorer students who wouldn't normally have a chance to go to Loyola. Read Father Steve Katsouros' moving book and you'll find that the new college worked by any measure (and that it was very, very hard). So . . . why not many more such places?"

—Donald E. Graham, co-founder of TheDream.US

"This captivating book introduces yet another Jesuit educational innovation, one with the potential to transform the world. It's an amazing story of Arrupe College's commitment to helping the next and future generations flourish."

—Honorable M. John Berry,
former United States Ambassador to Australia

Come to Believe

Dear Damian,
with admiration,
affection, + appreciation —
Since 1982.

Come to Believe

How the Jesuits Are Reinventing Education (Again)

Inside the First Year
of the New Arrupe College

Stephen N. Katsouros, SJ

ORBIS BOOKS

Maryknoll, New York 10545

ORBIS BOOKS
Maryknoll, New York 10545

Fathers and Brothers
MARYKNOLL™

Founded in 1970, Orbis Books endeavors to publish works that enlighten the mind, nourish the spirit, and challenge the conscience. The publishing arm of the Maryknoll Fathers and Brothers, Orbis seeks to explore the global dimensions of the Christian faith and mission, to invite dialogue with diverse cultures and religious traditions, and to serve the cause of reconciliation and peace. The books published reflect the views of their authors and do not represent the official position of the Maryknoll Society. To learn more about Maryknoll and Orbis Books, please visit our website at www.maryknollsociety.org.

Copyright © 2017 by Stephen N. Katsouros, SJ

Published by Orbis Books, Box 302, Maryknoll, NY 10545-0302.

All rights reserved. No part of this publication may be reproduced or transmitted in any form or by any means, electronic or mechanical, including photocopying, recording, or any information storage or retrieval system, without prior permission in writing from the publisher.

Queries regarding rights and permissions should be addressed to Orbis Books, P.O. Box 302, Maryknoll, NY 10545-0302.

Manufactured in the United States of America.

All student names have been changed to protect their privacy.

Library of Congress Cataloging-in-Publication Data

Names: Katsouros, Stephen N., author.
Title: Come to believe : how the Jesuits are reinventing education (again) : inside the first year of the new Arrupe College / Stephen N. Katsouros, SJ.
Description: Maryknoll, N.Y. : Orbis Books, 2017. | Includes index.
Identifiers: LCCN 2017005056 (print) | LCCN 2017020870 (ebook) | ISBN 9781608336852 (e-book) | ISBN 9781626982208 (pbk.)
Subjects: LCSH: Arrupe College (Chicago, Ill.) | College attendance—Social aspects—Illinois—Chicago. | College attendance—Economic aspects—Illinois—Chicago. | Community and college—Illinois—Chicago. | Jesuits—Education (Higher)—Illinois—Chicago.
Classification: LCC LD6501.A68 (ebook) | LCC LD6501.A68 K38 2017 (print) | DDC 378.1/5430977311—dc23
LC record available at https://lccn.loc.gov/2017005056

To my parents, Suzette and Nick Katsouros, my first teachers in the way of faith.

And to the students of Arrupe College, the best of teachers, whose witness has increased my faith.

God is the giver of all life, human and divine.
May God bless the parents of this child.
They will be the first teachers in the way of faith.
May they also be the best of teachers
Bearing witness to the faith by what they say and do,
In Christ Jesus our Lord. Amen.
—FROM THE BLESSING OF PARENTS DURING
THE CATHOLIC SACRAMENT OF BAPTISM

Contents

Part 3
The School
Building a New Model of Jesuit Higher Education

Part 4
The Students
Building a Culture of Accompaniment and Belonging

Acknowledgments

What was I thinking?

Writing a first book while starting a new college did not exactly make for compatible activities.

The writing of *Come to Believe* would have been impossible were it not for three individuals.

Early on, I decided to tackle this project by recording a series of vignettes about Arrupe College--our students, my experiences, our growth, our setbacks, my interior life. I thought recording would capture my voice, would feel more immediate (if less writerly), and would perhaps prove to be easier in the midst of a startup. Easier happened because of my Holy Trinity.

Jeremy Langford proved to be an invaluable sounding board about this process. He spent immeasurable amounts of time hearing me out and assisting me with creative ideas and later in the process with writing and revising. What's more, his wife (my classmate from theology) Liz Collier and he patiently, efficiently, effectively transcribed hours upon hours of tapes recorded in my office at night, during weekends, when I was exhausted, excited, exhilarated. As my mother would say, Liz and Jeremy have earned their crowns in heaven. The transmitter of those tapes was my administrative assistant, Wendolyn Gomez, who deployed her skills and smarts and considered ways to make the process easier and more accessible for Orbis Books, for Liz and Jeremy, and for me.

In Luke's Gospel, Gabriel declares to Mary, "Nothing is impossible with God." In my case, nothing was impossible because of Jeremy, Liz, and Wendolyn. Many thanks, and many blessings.

Preface

"I Know the Plans I Have for You"

*Yes, I know what plans I have in mind for you, plans for peace,
not for disaster, to give you a future and a hope.*
—JEREMIAH 29:11

On July 31, 2015, the Feast of St. Ignatius Loyola, Arrupe College completed its three-week Summer Enrichment Program (SEP) with mass at Madonna della Strada, the university church at Loyola University Chicago. Students and faculty, families and staff, board members and friends gathered to celebrate a marker in the beginnings of Loyola University's new enterprise: a two-year junior-college program that creates access for students who otherwise could never afford a Jesuit liberal arts education. After communion, we awarded two students, members of our inaugural class, Victoria and Khalil, with the Persons for Others awards, acknowledging our heritage and our patron, Fr. Pedro Arrupe. Fr. Arrupe, the superior general of the Society of Jesus (1965–83), gave Jesuit education its battle cry, its mission, its *raison d'être* of producing women and men for others.

During the summer Victoria had provided a brave and persistent voice for undocumented students during orientation sessions (*summer enrichment program* is our way to describe student orientation), advocating and asking questions that those in the shadows because of their status were uncomfortable to ask. Khalil, a Muslim, exercised tremendous care for another Muslim student who was struggling with fasting during Ramadan. In addition, Khalil exhibited empathy for classmates struggling

xiii

with academics in the classes that we offered during our summer enrichment program. I imagined St. Ignatius Loyola and Pedro Arrupe smiling down from heaven at all of us in Madonna della Strada Chapel on the feast of the founder as we presented a Muslim with a Person for Others award.

August was a mad dash as we scrambled to prepare for our opening on August 17, 2015. We planned to begin classes with the 159 young people who had participated in the July summer program and were now focused on becoming Arrupe's inaugural class, the class of 2017. Arrupe occupies the first three floors of Maguire Hall on Loyola University Chicago's Water Tower campus, in the city's downtown. Previously the location of Loyola's Quinlan School of Business, Maguire Hall is an outstanding building, in an even more outstanding location, a block away from the intersection of Chicago and State, a major transportation hub for the city of Chicago. The location is key to our success and key to success for our students, all of whom are commuters. During those weeks in August while we were moving into Maguire, I was also meeting with board members as we were getting ready to launch the school and talking to campus partners at Loyola University Chicago about the needs of our students who are also parents. How would these teenagers navigate childcare and their undergraduate educations? It was a hectic time.

In the midst of this activity, I received an email from Jim Keane, whom I had met while we were both working at the University of San Francisco. Jim is an editor at the venerable Catholic publishing house Orbis Books, and he had a question: Would I be willing to write a book covering the opening of Arrupe College and its first year? "Oy," I thought. I wasn't sure when I would brush my teeth during this first year, let alone write a book! So I tried stalling: "We are just launching this school, so why don't you wait until we have a year or two under our belts, until we have retained a class, until we have graduated a class, until we have placed a class in four-year colleges, once they have earned their associate's degree with us at Arrupe College? Why don't you wait until our first class graduates with bachelor's degrees?"

Jim was insistent, however, and asked me to give it serious consideration.

I spoke with another Jim: my friend Fr. Jim Martin, SJ. He and I met over twenty-five years ago, when we studied philosophy together at Loyola University Chicago as part of our Jesuit formation for the priesthood. Jim is the prolific and extraordinary award-winning author of many books, including *My Life with the Saints* and *The Jesuit Guide to (Almost) Everything*. I ran Jim Keane's invitation to write a book about the opening of Arrupe College by him. And, of course, I explained my reservations and my fears. Jim, however, would hear nothing of it. "You have to write this book," he said.

"But Jim," I reasoned, "this would be a much better book once we have some results, once we have some outcomes."

Jim's response was great. "Steve, what would be a more interesting read—a book written by St. Ignatius Loyola around 1540 when he and the first companions were launching the Society of Jesus, or a book one hundred years later looking back at the history of the Society and its founding?" Of course, the former would be the more compelling read. That's the book that all of us would like to read. He had me.

My usual style is to consult with people, so I spoke with one of our board members who was in the midst of writing his own book and asked him what he thought I should do. He said, "Yes, this is going to be killer for you. You are starting something new, you've got to raise a lot of money, but this is why you have to do it, because you will gain more funding and more support and more enthusiasm and attention for Arrupe College with this book. It's your vehicle for advancing Arrupe College's cause."

I called Jim Keane at Orbis. "OK," I said, resigned to my fate. "I'm in."

Taking on this book is consistent, I suppose, with who I am. Let me give an example. In the spring of 2016 my colleagues at Loyola University Chicago—the council of deans and the president's cabinet—and I participated in an exercise at the university during which a consulting firm assessed our leadership styles. My leadership style was identified as "dominant." Hmmm, I wondered, is that good? The dominant mode of leadership, according to the consultants and their assessment instrument, involves being pioneering and resolute, taking action, challenging oneself and others, having self-confidence, being forceful, and being willing to take risks. That seems to make sense in terms of my role as the founding dean at Arrupe College.

Arrupe College is indeed a pioneering activity. It has required tremendous persistence by our faculty and staff, by our students as they co-pioneer with us, and by the larger university community. Loyola University Chicago and I have been very active in implementing this idea that originated from Loyola's then-president Fr. Michael Garanzini, SJ, who envisioned this new educational movement that is so relevant, so compelling, and so necessary. Why wouldn't I, why wouldn't we as colleagues in Jesuit higher education, attempt this new way to make higher education accessible to those who otherwise would not have access?

Having a dominant leadership style, according to the assessment from the consulting team, also means being innovative. I'm in my late fifties now, and throughout my life as a Jesuit I've been able to engage in innovative ministries. Immediately before coming to Arrupe College, I served as the director of the University of San Francisco's Institute for Catholic Educational Leadership, known as ICEL. The Institute enjoyed a deservedly wonderful reputation for training and supporting Catholic educators, administrators, and scholars since its founding in the

1970s. What I wanted to bring to ICEL was something new and needed—professional development programs focused on trusteeship in Catholic education. During my years as director we created conferences for boards of high schools, colleges, and universities. I also gave presentations around the country to trustees of Catholic institutions—an innovation for ICEL.

Prior to engaging in post-secondary education, I served as president of Loyola School, a Jesuit high school on Manhattan's Upper East Side. I was Loyola's president for nine years, and I like to think of that as an innovative period for the school. Our team was able to honor the past and celebrate the leaders at Loyola School who came before us; at the same time, we collaborated to implement changes that moved Loyola forward into the independent school world of NYC while retaining what set us apart, what made us unique, what was key to our business model—our Jesuit and Catholic identity. We professionalized our roles; we reorganized the organizational chart; we became a higher-performing, more strategic board, and I believe that these changes helped us better meet the needs and expectations of our students and their families.

Earlier in my ministry I taught at Nativity schools, middle schools for students from low-income backgrounds. As a scholastic, a Jesuit in training, I was part of a team consisting of another Jesuit and a layman that started a Nativity school in Harlem called the Gonzaga Program at St. Aloysius School. Those times in the 1980s and 1990s were very creative for me: learning Spanish, developing confidence as a teacher, taking risks in terms of curriculum choices, building a culture at an entirely new apostolate, recruiting and supporting and accompanying new faculty. All of these experiences are part of the trajectory of the last thirty years that led to my assignment as dean and executive director of Arrupe College.

I was first approached by Mike Garanzini in the spring of 2014 to consider coming to Loyola University Chicago as the first dean of Arrupe. As I read Mike's enthusiastic email, I wondered if at this stage in my life, I could take on another startup. The Nativity school in Harlem was a startup, but I was in my thirties then. Despite the sobering reflection on my aging process, I also felt deep down that I had to take on this new challenge for the sake of the mission.

So many of us working in colleges and universities are concerned about the affordability of our institutions. We are concerned about issues of access, who is able to attend and compete at a Jesuit higher education institution, and who feels unwelcome or unable to make it in a Jesuit college or university. Even though I knew that this would be demanding work, I also had a hunch that it would be equally exciting and at times exhilarating. That dominant personality of mine surfaced, I suppose.

I was ordained in 1998. On my mass card I had printed this quotation from Jeremiah 29:11, "Yes, I know what plans I have in mind for you, plans for peace, not for disaster, to give you a future and a hope." When I said yes to Mike Garanzini's invitation and when my provincial said yes to assigning me as dean of Arrupe College, I didn't quite see this as God's plan for me. And yet, a year into Arrupe College, it is quite clear to me that this is what God intends for me to be part of during this chapter of my life.

Of course, it's not all about me. It's about the Arrupe College community—plans for peace for our students, not disaster; to give this educational movement a future; to give young people in Chicago more hope. Jeremiah's words well represent my mission, our mission, for the students of Arrupe College: "Yes, I know what plans I have in mind for you. Plans for peace, not for disaster. To give you a future and a hope."

Introduction

Come to Believe

*"Who are you?" Jesus answered, "What have I told you from
the outset? About you I have much to say and much to judge;
but the one who sent me is true, and I declare to the world
what I have learned from him." They did not recognize that
he was talking about the Father, so Jesus said, "When you
have lifted up the Son of Man, then you will know that I am
he and that I do nothing of my own accord but what I say is
what the Father has taught me. He who sent me is with me;
he has not left me to myself. I always do what pleases him."
As he was saying this, many came to believe in him.*

—JOHN 8:25–30

Before each board meeting for Arrupe College, I celebrate
mass at Baumhart Hall, the Loyola Chicago student residence hall where I live, directly across the street from Arrupe
College. Mass is not mandatory, but many of our board members
attend, as do a number of my colleagues from the college. On
Tuesday, March 15, 2016, at such a mass during Lent, the gospel
reading was from John 8:25–30, the passage cited above.

The line at the end of the gospel—"As he was saying this,
many came to believe in Him"—has truly been an anchor for
me in my adulthood. Later in John's Gospel, when Lazarus dies,
Martha says to Jesus, "I have come to believe in you." And Peter,
representing the apostles, says, "We have come to believe in you."

"We have come to believe" is such a powerful phrase. It does
not describe a single instant, because it has movement. It's fluid.
It's dynamic. It's gradual.

Faith, at least my experience of faith, is a process, not a lightning bolt, not a burning bush, not a eureka moment. We come to believe, and we grow in our faith. I love the dynamic, and it has given me great consolation to recognize that I don't have to get it right away. Faith is a lifelong process; we are works in progress.

In John's Gospel the sin Jesus encounters most often is unbelief. In celebrating mass with the board members that day, I explained that the sin I've experienced at Arrupe College is that a lot of people don't believe in our students. Well, since they don't know the students themselves, maybe it's fairer to say they don't believe in our demographic: those who come from a low-income background, who received okay-but-not-great grades in high school, whose ACT scores are mediocre at best, who come from the "other side of the tracks." Others may feel uncomfortable with or, worse, biased against young people of color. So the sin I see all too often is that those who are established and enjoy a certain privilege don't believe in our students.

And yet, something beautiful is happening with those students. To paraphrase those lines from John's Gospel, our students are coming to believe in themselves.

In walking the halls of Arrupe College, I see two students, Carlos and Omar, working on their statistics homework. Another student, Stephanie, talked earlier this year about how she loves statistics. Their classmate Carla has talked about how she loves math and treats it like a game that takes time to master. I love this type of resilience.

Some of our students dream about using their Arrupe College education to go on to Loyola University. Others hope to attend an out-of-state college when they complete their associate's degree with us. Some speculate about going on for medical training, for an MBA, for a law degree, for a PhD. The students have come to believe in themselves.

My homily with the board members that day centered on how important it is for us to show the students that we believe in them, that we believe that they belong in college, at Arrupe, at a Jesuit college.

We have come to believe. The students have come to believe. Again, this has been a huge anchor for me. The gradual process of creating and being part of this team, of building Arrupe College, of being at the beginning of something so important, of running a startup—as exhausting as it is—is all part of our coming to believe that we can do this. We have come to believe an unlikely proposition: that we can make a high-quality, Jesuit post-secondary liberal arts education affordable, accessible, and achievable for young people from low-income backgrounds. *We have come to believe.*

PART 1

Mission to Educate

My Jesuit Journey

Not Doing For, Being With

Understanding My White Privilege

"Martha, Martha," the Lord answered, "you are worried and upset about many things, but few things are needed—or indeed only one. Mary has chosen what is better, and it will not be taken away from her."
—LUKE 10:41–42

Before I tell another word of this story, I want to acknowledge that I am keenly aware that I am a privileged white male. To help me understand my privilege, I reflect on the sisters we encounter in Luke's Gospel—multitasking Martha and meditative Mary. This link may seem a little out of left field, so let me explain.

As dean of Arrupe College, a post-secondary institution where 97 percent of the students are people of color, I am conscious of my status as an exceedingly privileged, middle-aged white man. I don't think that my experience of being the first from my family to attend college qualifies me to see myself like an Arrupe student—I don't impose my experience as universal. I am grateful for the opportunities I've enjoyed to study and eventually to earn four master's degrees and a doctorate. (My mother once observed, "These diplomas, they're like baseball cards for you.") I am proud of my achievements, but my history is not a playbook for our students. Rather, I enjoy hearing about their experiences and aspirations. In fact, I'm inspired by their stories.

Back to white privilege. Earlier this year a diverse group of Arrupe supporters and I discussed job placement for our students. I'm frustrated that more of our students aren't able to work. Approximately 20 percent of our students are undocumented, and accompanying them through the Scylla and Charybdis of attaining an Employment Authorization Document (EAD) makes real for me the desperate need for immigration reform in this country. Other students struggle with the pressures of long commutes, childcare and other family demands, as well as the need to focus on courses at Arrupe. Our schedule is very structured and predictable—students take courses during mornings or afternoons Mondays, Tuesdays, Thursdays, and Fridays. The design is deliberate; we don't want Arrupe to contribute to the dismal statistic that only 5 percent of students enrolled in two-year programs graduate in two years. Put another way, we want Arrupe students to be members of the 5 percent club. Yet, the focus, structure, and emphasis on daily contact with students, beneficial as they have been to our overall retention rate, can get in the way of our students finding a job. Those who do find jobs that they can navigate end up working in fast-food restaurants and retail stores. My fear, however, is that our students will plateau at Taco Bell or Nordstrom Rack, that their horizons don't include knowing many people in professions like finance or in the STEM (science, technology, engineering, math) fields.

The conversation with our Arrupe supporters surfaced these tensions. A number of the participants who share my demographic talked about internships as a method of bolstering our students' resumes. Unpaid internships could open doors, they reasoned, by offering networking opportunities and exposure to white-collar professional settings.

One of the discussion participants, an African American man, shook his head. "Internships are a luxury Arrupe students can't afford," he said. "They need money now, to help their mothers make rent, to help buy groceries, to cover their own immediate expenses." The scales fell from our eyes. The unpaid internship, an effective strategy for one demographic, didn't apply to another. For Arrupe students the model for growth and opportunity is not one size fits all.

Along these same lines, I am increasingly aware of how "microaggressions"—expressions by those who enjoy privilege that unintentionally dismiss and degrade women, people of color, gays and lesbians, and people with disabilities—tumble out of my mouth or the mouths of others.

During a discussion about Arrupe's mission statement, for example, one of the participants said, "We don't have any language about 'saving the students.'" The remark was made benignly, generously, but I still dug in my heels. "Let's let Jesus save," I replied. "That's his job." Saving our students smacked of a savior complex, or colonialism, or worse.

During another discussion, with a campus ministry professional, I discussed the possibility of Arrupe students participating in an alternative spring break immersion trip to Appalachia to build houses and work in soup kitchens while reflecting on the factors that cause people to lack food, clothes, and shelter. The campus minister expressed some reservations. "I wonder," she said, "if Arrupe students are really up for the task, if they are mature enough to be away from home." Then she added innocently, sincerely, "Other students spend time during the immersion trip grappling with issues of social injustice. Would the Arrupe students be able to do that?"

"Hmmm," I began. "Before our conversation, I met with Luisa, a student with a 4.0 average at Arrupe whose father was just deported. That's a level of maturity that awes me." My indignation spurred me to continue, "Interesting point you made about being away from home. Five of our students are homeless, so they are very accustomed to being away from home." I concluded by observing, "As for grappling with issues of social injustice, this isn't just an abstract concept that our students might visit for a week. It's all they know."

Service projects aside, when I floated the whole idea of Arrupe College by an accomplished higher-education leader, he said, "We considered doing that at my institution, but the faculty pushed back. 'Those students, the ones who attend community colleges,' they said, 'they're not the same caliber as our students. If they became a part of our college, they would diminish our brand.'" In response to my friend's pitch to incorporate a community college in an economically depressed neighborhood into their university, they instead offered to serve as volunteers at the community college, but to keep it at that.

Back to Martha and Mary. Frequently when I'm giving a talk during an Arrupe student town hall, I repeat author Robert Greenleaf's mantra, "To serve is to lead, to lead is to serve." My understanding of why I serve and how to serve has grown since my own college and post-college experiences led me to join the Society of Jesus. Martha and Mary are a part of that evolution.

I am a fan of Martha. Martha is real in her emotions—she loves Jesus enough to be honest with him about her disappointment in him. In John's Gospel, when her brother Lazarus dies, she expresses anger at Jesus for not showing up. And Martha's insight, that "she has come to believe" that Jesus is Lord, succinctly and profoundly captures our faith journey, one that is gradual and ongoing.

My experience at Arrupe informs my appreciation and appropriation of Martha and Mary in Luke's Gospel—the overwrought hostess and the sister sitting at the feet of Jesus. Martha is doing for Jesus; Mary is being with Jesus. Our mission at Arrupe is not so much *doing for* our students, particularly when our white privilege results in damaging and deadening microaggressions. Our mission is *being with* our students, learning about and from them, sharing our stories and the gift of Jesuit higher education. The best ministerial strategies of the Society of Jesus—inculturation, learning about and celebrating the cultures of those we are assigned to serve—stem from *being with*, as Mary exemplifies by being with Jesus.

Don't Be Afraid

The best moments in life are those that you don't anticipate.
—ARRUPE STUDENT

When I celebrate mass, I often preach about what's happening at Arrupe. In fact, I preach about Arrupe whenever anyone is willing to listen!

The first time that I gave a homily about Arrupe College was about a month before I moved to Chicago to take on my new assignment leading the new school. I was on Cape Cod, celebrating mass for Arrupe board member Mark Shriver and his family on the fifth anniversary of the death of Mark's mother, Eunice Kennedy Shriver, the founder of Special Olympics. The gospel reading for that day was Matthew 14:22–33, the Calming of the Storm, in which Jesus says to Peter and the disciples, "Take courage. It is I. Do not be afraid." As I get older, the encouragement from Jesus to let go of fear becomes increasingly meaningful.

When I preach, I'm often preaching to myself. During that mass on the Cape, I was deep in transition. I was leaving the University of San Francisco and heading to Chicago to launch Arrupe College. I had no idea if this project would take off or not. It kept churning in my mind that this was the Society of Jesus's first junior college for under-represented students. "We have to get this right for these students," I fretted. "I have to get this right."

Besides my anxieties driving my preaching content, I was also aware this was Eunice Shriver's anniversary. During the mass I recalled seeing Mrs. Shriver ten years before at a lunch at the William Simon Foundation in New York, during which she received a half-million-dollar gift for Special Olympics. Eunice Shriver's message to her special friends with intellectual disabilities echoed Jesus's charge to the disciples—do not be afraid. Don't be afraid to be an athlete, Mrs. Shriver had said. Don't be afraid to go to school. Don't be afraid to pursue a job. Don't be afraid.

I found her message an inspiration as I was contemplating my new assignment, and I shared that feeling with Mrs. Shriver's children and grandchildren. I talked about the students that we were anticipating at Arrupe, students from low-income back-grounds who are the first in their families to attempt college. I reflected on their fears about belonging (or not) in Jesuit higher education. I imagined the similarities between the disciples on the tempest-tossed boat in the Gospel and the students who feel the winds pushing against them—winds of injustice, of prejudice, of lack of opportunity, of lack of access. I then described my role as dean of Arrupe College as one who would say to our students, "Take courage. Do not be afraid." Of course, my exhortation was directed at myself, as I was taking on a new apostolate, relocating to a new city, starting a new job and chapter in my life, learning how to navigate new demands on me. To all of this Jesus says, "Do not be afraid."

In the Gospel, Peter steps into the unknown and is vulnerable. We are called to do the same, and we are also called to stretch out our hands to catch those who are vulnerable and say to one another, "Don't be afraid." In starting Arrupe College my prayer has focused on this theme. We are building God's kingdom and putting aside our fears and addressing our students' fears, concerns, and disappointments about not getting into a four-year college, about not having the financial resources to attend a four-year college, about not feeling worthy of college. Together with the students, I imagined Jesus saying to them and to me, "Do not be afraid." Together with the students, Jesus invited them and me, and our fears, to the next chapter of our lives.

Cura Personalis—
Care for the Whole Person

After the first meeting I attended at Arrupe, I clearly saw how motivated, excited, and driven Arrupe was for the students to be successful. With their inclusive spirit, they wanted every person to feel wanted. That was what I needed going into my first year of college, a support team. I could see that ever single staff and faculty truly cared for my well-being and my success, and that is why I chose Arrupe.

                —ARRUPE STUDENT

A dear friend of mine in New York, Michael Angelo Allocca, died recently at the age of eighty-one. I saw him for the last time when I was home at Christmastime in 2015. Mike suffered from Alzheimer's, and when he died, his family asked if I would preach at his funeral at their parish, St. Francis Xavier, in the Chelsea section of Manhattan. I go back thirty-five years with Mike, his wife, Rose, and their sons. We met shortly after I completed my year as a member of the Jesuit Volunteer Corps, often called JVC. I often introduced Rose and Mike Allocca as my Brooklyn parents.

My biological parents, Suzette and Nick Katsouros, had been very concerned at the time about me joining JVC. Earlier, during my freshman year at the University of Maryland, I had thrown my parents a curve ball when I told them I wanted to major in English. "English?" my father, the son of Greek immigrants, asked. "You speak English. Why are you majoring in English?" During my years at Maryland, while I was reading Chaucer and Shakespeare, Flannery O'Connor and Toni Morrison, and while my parents' eyes were rolling, I also engaged in several service activities, a practice inculcated from programs in which I participated during high school. It was no surprise to anyone, then—except my parents—when I applied to the JVC for a year of service. "JVC?" my father asked before I could explain what the acronym stood for. "You know nothing about stereo equipment. You majored in English. How can you work for JVC?"

JVC missioned me to serve as a childcare worker at Covenant House, in New York's Times Square. During a JVC midyear retreat, I listened to a presentation by Jesuit Fr. Dean Brackley on Ignatian spirituality. I had not attended Jesuit schools before, so Dean's references to "finding God in all things" and striving to become "contemplatives in action" caught my attention powerfully.

So did ministry at Covenant House, a center for homeless youth. There I experienced the frustration of making progress with people a few years younger than me through counseling and conversations about faith, hope, and a better future, only to see everything come crashing down when a young man went AWOL or a young woman's thirty-day tenure at Covenant House ended. During those days I thought about my own need for predictability, for community. As my JVC year was drawing to a close, I looked for a new ministry. I wasn't a Jesuit and wasn't considering a vocation to the Jesuits, but I admired Dean Brackley and other Jesuits I had met during JVC.

Dean Brackley had been a founder of Nativity Mission School in the early 1970s, ten years before I met him. After JVC, in 1982, I began teaching at Nativity, located at 204 Forsyth St. on Manhattan's Lower East Side. Nativity was the first of what became the Nativity Miguel model schools. In the 1970s, prior to my move to Forsyth Street, Jesuits like Dean and laypeople there recognized that the public schools in District 1 missed the mark when it came to meeting the needs and celebrating the strengths of the children and grandchildren of immigrants. The Lower East Side had served as the cradle of newcomers to New York for over a century. The neighborhood has been gentrified in recent years and is now the cradle of boutique hotels and high-end restaurants and clubs. Displaced from this area are the Puerto Ricans and Dominicans and Mexicans I knew during my five years of living and working there, immigrants and the children of immigrants who dwelled in the tenements on Eldridge, Rivington, Pitt, Stanton, and Houston Streets, or the public housing projects along the FDR Drive.

The students enrolled at Nativity hailed from these projects and tenements. Nativity was an all-boys middle school (sixth, seventh, and eighth grades) that included a leadership-training summer camp in Lake Placid. Mike and Rose Allocca were very involved with Nativity. Rose, an accomplished teacher and administrator at Brooklyn Tech High School, volunteered at Nativity and eventually served as Nativity's principal. Mike, a successful New York financier, hosted many dinners at various restaurants in Brooklyn and Manhattan; Mike said his ministry was to feed hungry Jesuits.

When I met Rose and Mike, I wasn't a Jesuit yet. I taught and lived on the Lower East Side in an apartment with other faculty at Nativity for five years, from 1982 to 1987. I entered the Society of Jesus because of my experience of ministry, my students, and the Jesuits at Nativity. I was inspired by Jesuits like Dean Brackley and Ed Durkin, who served as director of

Nativity. The meals out with Mike and Rose may have been inspirational, too.

Living with and working with and for the people of the Lower East Side in the 1980s also inspired me. In the projects kids just ten or eleven years old made quick money running nickel bags of pot. They could help their mothers with rent or groceries or buy basketball shoes or a new coat. This was a far more immediate satisfaction of needs than studying grammar and diagramming sentences with me or learning algebra taught by Ed Durkin.

Gangs were a presence on the Lower East Side, along with pushers. Young people who aged out of services offered at places like Covenant House found their way downtown from Times Square to homeless shelters on East Third Street and to the food, kindness, and beds at the Catholic Worker houses. In closest proximity, however, were prostitutes, working across the street from Nativity at Sara Delano Roosevelt Park. The Nativity students and faculty knew the prostitutes, some by name, because of their constant presence on our block. The prostitutes, mostly teenagers, were marching to their deaths from overdoses and AIDS. My colleagues at Nativity could track the progress of drug addiction or the virus on the faces of these girls as they lost more and more weight and then as they disappeared from Forsyth Street.

One morning I could tell my students in grammar class were not exactly engrossed by the lesson on identifying parts of speech. They were following some loud commotion outside. Maria, a prostitute who was likely no older than sixteen, was shrieking f-bombs at her pimp. I stuck my head out the window of my classroom and shouted, "Hey, Maria, can you take this down the street?" Maria and the pimp looked up. "Oh, Steve, okay, no problem," she replied. As Maria and the pimp proceeded south on Forsyth Street, the f-bombs faded. Back to parts of speech.

In circumstances like these I marveled at the resilience of my students and their capacity to travel in the world of a Jesuit school and the world of the street. I also shuddered to think of how much they carried inside, how much they saw and experienced and knew already in middle school. Another time I witnessed a prostitute stabbing her pimp on a Friday afternoon as our students left classes and headed to Sara Delano Roosevelt Park to play. The pimp was bleeding all over the Nativity car Ed Durkin used to drive students home after evening study hall. I remember trying to distract the students from the sight, as if they hadn't seen similar scenes last month, last week, last night.

When I first arrived at Nativity, I was concerned that there weren't many books in our library. But eight blocks north, on 2nd Avenue and Saint Mark's Place, was a branch of the New York Public Library. So I tried an experiment with two of my students, Willie and Raymond. I tried to convince them that the library was a wonderful place that we should visit. "The library has books that match any possible interest you might have," I said with enthusiasm. "It has all kinds of resources, and there are librarians who are nice and helpful."

Willie and Raymond listened to me as if I were describing another planet, not a location that was a ten-minute walk north, but they were game to see what the library was all about. We walked up 2nd Avenue, discussing their interests, what kinds of books they might check out. Once inside the library we were greeted by staff members who were happy to help. We also noted that the library served as a haven for the homeless and for those who suffer from mental illness.

Martial arts captivated Willie, so we began to search that section of the shelves. As we began to register Raymond and Willie for library cards, someone grabbed me and started pummeling me, yelling, "I told you not to do that, I told you not to do that." I had inadvertently brushed against this person, which apparently offended him. As I dodged swings, I realized he was ill, he was suffering. (So was I—my eye had begun to swell.) Rather than becoming defensive, I said, "You're right. I'm wrong. I'm sorry, I should not have done that."

His rage subsided, and he walked away from Willie, Raymond, and my black eye. My students looked sick. So much for all of my rhetoric about how great libraries are, I thought. "We hate this place," they said. "Who wants to go to the library and watch your teacher get beaten up?" I stumbled back down 2nd Avenue with a swollen eye and a throbbing head and shuffled into Nativity Mission Center. Ed Durkin was counseling one of our students. He looked up at me and said, "What the hell happened to you, Steve? Where have you been?" I gave the short answer: "the library."

My five years at Nativity served as my training ground for the Jesuit concept of *cura personalis*—care for the whole person. My colleagues lived above the school in the tenement that housed Nativity. We knew the blocks and buildings of our students. We spent time with them after school, evenings in study hall, summers at Nativity's camp in Lake Placid. We interacted with their families. Willie, my library companion, grew into a volatile young man, especially after his mother died of AIDS. Willie lived with an overwhelmed grandmother, and he carried a gun. He didn't graduate from Nativity. Instead, he visited the school once, brandishing his pistol. I ran after him on Forsyth Street to see if something I could do or say would make a difference, would reach him somehow. I wasn't able to catch up with him that afternoon.

Several years later I was walking on the Lower East Side and spotted Willie pushing a toddler in a stroller. I had heard he had married a girl named Carolina and they were the parents of a little boy. Bumping into Willie transported me to the grammar classes I had taught at Nativity. I had used a textbook called *Drill for Skill* that the students dubbed "Kill for Skill." We diagrammed sentences and put together endless writing and public-speaking and book-publishing exercises. As Willie and I greeted each other and I met his son in the stroller, I recalled that Willie was one of the less engaged students.

Willie volunteered, "You know, I'm teaching Carolina what you taught us, Mr. K." I wasn't sure where this was going and asked, "What do you mean, Willie?" He answered, "I still have my copy of the *Drill for Skill* book we used. Remember, 'Kill for Skill'? I'm teaching her the parts of speech." I was dumbfounded. "Get outta here," I said. "We were in class together seven years ago. No way." Willie insisted, "No, look." He pulled out his old assignment notebook. "Now see, Mr. K, Carolina and me, we're working on personal pronouns, because you taught us that in October of 1982." This completely floored me. There was no reason for Willie to carry this artifact from seven years before. He had relocated repeatedly since then, and his life was very unpredictable. But he hung onto that textbook because it meant something to him.

Although Willie had not graduated from Nativity, many students did. But the big question at the time was, "Now what?" To address this question my friend Rose Allocca and I initiated Nativity's Graduate Support Program in 1984. By then, Nativity had been enrolling classes and graduating eighth graders for over ten years. My predecessors and contemporaries at Nativity and I found our commitment to *cura personalis* had been successful, but student confidence unraveled when they transitioned to high schools with higher enrollments, and in some cases with a majority of white students. (Nativity began in part to assist the students in enrolling at and graduating from New York–area Jesuit or Catholic high schools.) Unless the Nativity graduates were academically excellent or athletic superstars or always in detention ("JUG" in Jesuit parlance), they could get lost. Even after going on to high school, they would often gravitate back to Nativity because it was home, in their neighborhood, because they had relationships with faculty, staff members, and administrators there. Nativity's Graduate Support Program began by offering tutoring and a special study hall at night for our graduates.

But we needed to do more. We wanted to collaborate with the parents of our students. This desire drove me to travel to the Dominican Republic to learn Spanish, since the majority of our students and their parents were Dominican. Upon my return my Spanish vocabulary and accent were almost comical, but the Nativity community was grateful that I attempted to learn their language. I would give presentations to the parents in mangled Spanish, but they would applaud. The important thing was that I developed enough of a vocabulary to communicate with the parents about how their sons were progressing academically or about the high school application process.

As part of the Graduate Support Program I started to accompany parents of Nativity graduates to parent-teacher conferences and other events at the high schools where their sons were attending. Magdalena, the mother of Julian, asked me once if I would attend a parents' association event with her at her son's high school. I was close to the family. Magdalena worked in a sweatshop not far from the family of seven's one-bedroom apartment. The high school event was a fashion show, and the other attendees intended to purchase what the models were wearing. Magdalena couldn't afford to do that but discovered another connection to what was presented on the runway: Magdalena had sewn the zippers on the dresses.

Another parent, Zilpa, also worked in a sweatshop. I wanted Zilpa to see how long the commute from the Lower East Side would take for her son Fernando to arrive at his high school uptown on time. The mothers and I would time the commute from the 2nd Avenue subway station near Nativity to the different schools. Zilpa, dressed in her Sunday best, and I traveled to Regis High School, the prestigious tuition-free prep school run by the Jesuits on New York's Upper East Side. When we arrived, some of the faculty members who were going to teach Fernando spoke with us. Some of them spoke Spanish, and they were very hospitable. Zilpa appreciated their kindness, but she was most taken with the flowers in the neighborhood where Fernando would go to school. Why? Because there were no flowers on the Lower East Side and no flowers in the sweatshop. I think that the next time Zilpa was at Regis was probably for Fernando's graduation, but she knew that he was in a safe environment, one very different from the one in which she lived. She trusted the Jesuits, she trusted the high school, she trusted Nativity, and I was honored that she trusted me. No *cura personalis,* no trust.

Pretend

Kids need heat and light to survive. Heat, in the form of respectful, dignified vigilance over them. Light, in the form of hope for some kind of future beyond this.
—Fr. Greg Boyle, SJ, Homeboy Industries

I entered the Society of Jesus in 1987. Part of our training, or formation, includes regency, two or three years of practical experience working in a Jesuit institution, typically a school, before advancing to theology studies. For my regency I was assigned to a team to start a middle school based on the Nativity model at St. Aloysius Parish in Harlem. I was reunited with Jesuit Fr. Ed Durkin from Nativity, who was such a huge influence on me before I entered the Society. Ed and I worked with a young African American man named Clyde Cole, who is now a good friend. Clyde graduated from Regis High School in New York and played basketball while attending Northwestern University.

Ed, Clyde, and I were the original team. We called the school the Gonzaga Program. I taught nine classes a day and raised money for scholarships and special projects. As we grew our student body and expanded our faculty by bringing in members of the Jesuit Volunteer Corps, I supervised them and worked on developing the school's curriculum. None of these earned me as much appreciation as another job: I was also the janitor that first year! I had another role that earned me almost no appreciation at all: I served as the master after classes in the JUG room, where students appeared when they received detention. (Countless alums of Jesuit schools believe JUG is an acronym for Justice Under God. In fact, JUG is a contraction of the Latin *iugere*, "to yoke," as an ox, for the purpose of manual labor, or punishment.) No one was happy in the JUG room.

I taught our writing course at the Gonzaga Program of St. Aloysius. Our classes were small by design. For one assignment I asked the fourteen students in my class to write about what a reunion would be like twenty years later. Who would be doing what? What high schools and colleges might they have attended? Where would they be living? Who would be married and raising a family?

Of course, I got caught up in what I thought would be a meaningful and enjoyable assignment for our close-knit class. I was brought back to earth when one of the students asked, in a very matter-of-fact manner, "Mr. K, what if you think you won't be alive twenty years from now?"

That gave me pause.

I remember having the presence of mind to simply say, "Pretend." But asking the students to pretend at the age of thirteen that they would be alive at the age of thirty-three revealed a startling fact: our students did not have a future orientation in Harlem. We began the Gonzaga Program in 1991, during the height of the crack epidemic, when gun violence was rampant.

Ed Durkin and I lived with two other Jesuits on West 132nd between 7th and 8th Avenues. When I first arrived and walked through the neighborhood, I was asked, "Are you lost?" I became accustomed to falling asleep at night with gunshots in the background: white noise. But the question from the students at the Gonzaga Program—what if you think you won't be alive twenty years from now?—has bothered me since the day I introduced a seemingly benign assignment in class. *Pretend.*

Don't Sell the Students Short

I've ultimately learned that although being an adult is rough, I can do it.

—Arrupe student

My relationship with the city of Chicago didn't begin with my time as dean and executive director of Arrupe College. After finishing two years at the Jesuit novitiate at St. Andrew Hall in Syracuse, the next phase of my Jesuit formation included two years of philosophy studies. My options were Fordham in the Bronx or Loyola University Chicago. I already had a master's degree from Fordham, which I had earned when I was working and teaching at Nativity. A close Jesuit friend of mine from the class ahead of me, Ed Cunningham, was in Chicago and liked his experience at Loyola. I talked to my superiors in New York and was assigned to Chicago.

It was a wonderful time. I didn't realize that I would like philosophy, but the department was very strong. I had terrific Jesuit instructors like Mark Henninger and Harry Gensler and Leo Sweeney, and lay instructors like Sue Cunningham and Patricia Werhane. And, of course, there was everyone's favorite, a BVM nun, Sr. Louise French, who was a wonderful friend to so many Jesuit scholastics. During that time, besides reconnecting with my friend Ed (who later left the Jesuits), I made a number of new friends, particularly two Jesuits: Karl Kiser, who recently finished his presidency at the University of Detroit Jesuit High School after fourteen years at the helm; and Gene Geinzer, who was already ordained and teaching in the Loyola Department of Fine Arts at the time and now is working and teaching in Beijing.

I was grateful for that time because it really expanded my horizons in the Society of Jesus. I had been focused on New York in that typical "there's no life west of the Hudson" way, and while I still have the strongest affinity to New York and consider New York home, I loved doing a "deep dive" into the Midwest, Chicago particularly. I was impressed by Chicago's architecture; neighborhoods; public transportation; food, sports, and arts scene; and affordability—especially compared to New York City.

I spent two years at Loyola Chicago studying philosophy and ended up getting a master's degree at Loyola before being assigned as a regent to begin the Gonzaga Program at St. Aloysius in Harlem. Karl Kiser and I reconnected in theology. Karl had served in Peru during his regency, where he met Fr. John Foley. When John returned to the United States after many, many years in Peru, he had the idea of beginning a new kind of inner-city school, called Cristo Rey, that would combine a work program with a strong Jesuit-inspired educational curriculum for disadvantaged students. Because of my work at the original Nativity and the startup Gonzaga Program, Karl told John to speak with me. So John made a trip to the Weston School of Theology (now part of Boston College) where Karl and I were living and studying. John traveled with Sr. Judy Murphy, a Benedictine sister. They were in the beginning stages of discerning a request made by then–Jesuit Provincial Brad Schaeffer for the Jesuits to better serve the Mexican immigrant families living in Chicago's

Pilsen neighborhood. The idea was to make Jesuit education more accessible through a new high school model that helped students pay for their education through a work-study program.

John, Judy, and I now laugh about this, but when they were describing the new school to me, I was very skeptical. "Why do the white students at Loyola Academy and St. Ignatius College Prep, the Jesuit high schools in the Chicago area, go to school five days a week, and the students from low-income backgrounds go to school only four days a week?" I asked. This was before Cristo Rey had an extended year and an extended school-day schedule. Then I asked John, "Now when these students graduate from Cristo Rey, you're preparing them to go to Harvard and University of Chicago and Northwestern and Stanford, right?" He responded, "Oh, my God, never, no way." And I said, "Okay, alright, they're going to go to Notre Dame and to Georgetown and Santa Clara, right?" And he said, "No, never. That's just not in the cards for them." So I said, "All right, they're going to go to Marquette and Loyola University, aren't they? And DePaul?" And he said, "No, they won't be doing that." So I said, "Well then, John, get out of it. Because we're Jesuits and we run college preps. This is a crazy idea and it'll never work."

Cristo Rey has been easily the most exciting and effective innovation that has happened in Catholic secondary education in the last twenty years. And all these years later many Cristo Rey graduates have gone on to graduate from all of those schools I had mentioned. So I'm willing to admit that if you're ever looking for someone to predict the success of a trend, don't ask me!

Cristo Rey, of course, was the beginning of what is now a network of thirty-two Cristo Rey model high schools around the country. I was delighted to be at a ceremony kicking off a new Cristo Rey in Milwaukee, and I'm honored to be on the board of directors of the original Cristo Rey in the Pilsen neighborhood of Chicago. And I'm relieved John Foley and Judy Murphy didn't heed my advice about their idea.

Leadership

Embracing the Good to Which We Are Called

Change will not come if we wait for some other person or some other time. We are the ones we've been waiting for. We are the change that we seek.

—BARACK OBAMA

Prior to engaging in post-secondary education, I served from 2002 to 2011 as president of Loyola School, a Jesuit high school on Manhattan's Upper East Side. As I mentioned earlier, during my tenure we were able to move the school forward in new ways while honoring its history and distinctive Jesuit and Catholic identity. The experience taught me a great deal about leadership and about my own leadership style in particular. If I had to boil it down, my leadership hinges on three main maxims.

The first maxim is knowing when to leave and to leave them wanting more. The celebration of my final vows (ultimate confirmation of membership in the Society of Jesus) on Ascension Thursday in early June 2011 served as my farewell from Loyola. It was very emotional but also affirming and wonderful. I felt I was leaving Loyola in very good shape. The kindness and support I experienced at Loyola combined powerfully with the many friendships I experienced through decades of ministry in New York. Consequently, my final vows in 2011, along with my first mass back in 1998, both at the Church of St. Ignatius Loyola in Manhattan, are spiritual and personal highlights for which I will always be deeply grateful. The liturgy of the final vows, attended by over a thousand people from various chapters of my life, felt movie-like. And, in terms of Loyola School, I left them wanting more. But it was time for me to move on to a new assignment. Accompanied by a dedicated community of students, colleagues, parents, alumni, and trustees, I had completed my assignment. I also finally had completed my doctorate at Teacher's College at Columbia University the previous April, and after prayer and discernment I had told my provincial superior I felt called to transition to administration in higher education.

The second maxim I strive to live by is that effective leadership is about paying attention to the right thing at the right time. My Jesuit friend Bob Reiser is a master at this. As president of McQuaid Jesuit High School in Rochester, New York, and before that as president at St. Peter's Prep in New Jersey, Bob has exhibited outstanding leadership by knowing where and when to focus his attention. Another Jesuit friend, Damian O'Connell, has taught me to recognize that there are many goods competing for our energy and attention, attempting to lay claims on us, and that one needs to ask, "What is the good to which I'm called?"

When I moved from teaching, which I truly loved, to respond to the call to serve in administration, I was very aware that I would have less immediate connection with students and the powerful daily formation that happens between students and their instructors. To accept the call I had to make some sacrifices so that I could focus my attention on collaborating with and contributing to a team that is moving an institution forward.

The third maxim that informs my leadership is that building the right team is the key to success, no matter what the task at hand is. This was a challenge I needed to address when I became president at Loyola in 2002, both internally and on the board level.

Eventually, with high-performing trustees and outstanding administrators in place, Loyola changed for the better. Three key hires advanced Loyola so that the school incarnated the book everyone seemed to be reading at that time, Jim Collins's *Good to Great*. Jim Lyness, long-time Loyola faculty leader and math department chair, returned to Loyola two years into my term and served as our academic head, or headmaster. Jim was and is an outstanding leader and deeply committed to Jesuit education and to inculcating the "grad at grad," a summary of the five characteristics of a graduate of a Jesuit high school at the time of graduation: open to growth, academic excellence, religious, loving, and committed to doing justice. Susan Conniff began in 2003 as our vice president for finance and was my "good right hand" in many ways. Susan's previous experience in finance at JP Morgan and her incredible work ethic so professionalized our business office that it served as a model for other Jesuit and independent school finance operations. Tony Oroszlany, a graduate of Loyola School, returned to his alma mater in 2003 as the vice president for advancement and is now the school's president. Smart and savvy, sensitive and pastoral, Tony was a "utility player" and a pleasure to work with. We worked very well together; Tony, thoughtful, careful, a researcher able to focus; and I, with my extroverted, risk-taking personality.

When we would ask individuals or couples or foundations for their financial support, Tony offered what I called "the stats," the financial perspective, while I gave "the story," describing the students, the need, the mission. Because of Tony's versatility, sometimes we would flip our routine. Tony attended Loyola on a scholarship, so he could share his experience of the school's impact on him. During my tenure at Loyola I befriended several other school presidents and heads and served on boards, which afforded me the opportunity to learn about best practices and how they might be adapted at Loyola, which I often discussed with prospective donors. Tony and I met and solicited support from many donors, but we were much more effective when our styles complemented each other's and we went on an "ask" together. The lessons I learned from the leadership team at Loyola School remain a driving force for me in my leadership of Arrupe College.

The main challenge at Arrupe is that we are creating a culture somewhat out of thin air. While Arrupe is a college within Loyola University Chicago, a very well-established educational institution that has been in existence since 1870, Arrupe is also brand new. For example, when someone suggests talking to our campus partners to address an issue, the reality is that our campus partners are accustomed to working with students who have ACT scores of 27 and GPAs of 3.7. Our students have an average ACT score of 18 and an average GPA of 2.5. So what works for some of our campus partners at Loyola does not work, or needs to be adapted, for Arrupe. My colleagues at Arrupe, especially our two associate deans, Jennie Boyle and Yolanda Golden, have exercised great sensitivity in adapting best practices at Loyola University to the needs and realities of Arrupe College.

Having Jennie Boyle as associate dean for academics and Yolanda Golden as associate dean for student success allows me to be externally focused, which I enjoy and find stimulating. A big part of that focus is fundraising. During Arrupe's first year we needed to raise about one million dollars. We supported thirty-five undocumented students, who were not receiving federal and state aid—approximately $10,000 per student. So we had to raise $350,000 for those students alone. We created a breakfast and lunch program at a cost of $150,000. We also give each of our students a laptop. That's over $100,000. And we give all of our students the opportunity to participate in the summer enrichment program, which again costs over $100,000. Assistance for immigrants, predictable and nutritious breakfasts and lunches, laptops, orientation (summer enrichment program)—these are what I call baseline services—the minimum students need in order to be successful at Arrupe, or anywhere. The baseline services added up. Providence occurred when a friend from New York, newlywed Maggie Murphy Stockson, moved to Chicago and expressed interest in working at Arrupe. As our assistant dean for advancement, Maggie drives our fund-raising efforts with passion and grace.

A big part of fundraising is saying thank you. I enjoy writing our donor-acknowledgment letters and have become well known through the years for crafting them myself with concrete examples of what's going on at the institutions I'm serving. At Arrupe, I might describe a scene of a class I observed or perhaps the achievement of a student. In one particular letter I spoke about our students preparing to make a retreat. Our retreat program at Arrupe is made possible because of a $100,000 donation we received from a foundation and is facilitated by one of our board members. I sign every letter, whether the gift is for $25 or $500,000. I usually scribble a personal message as well, indicating our gratitude for the donor's generosity.

I engage in similar practices with our students. Writing and receiving letters with handwritten messages is becoming archaic in our era of texts and tweets. Such letters, because they are going the way of all things, also capture one's attention, so I sign and send letters via "snail mail" to all students earning a GPA of 3.5 and meriting a place on the dean's list. I congratulate the students on their grades, and then I exhort them to continue their great work in their upcoming classes. Yes, it takes a lot of time to look at each student's record to see what courses the student took during the last semester and is enrolled in this semester, but it's worth it. Why? It demonstrates to the student that we are paying attention. It shows that we are interested in the student. It contributes to the culture of *cura personalis*.

On Super Bowl Sunday, February 7, 2016, I presided at the 5:00 p.m. mass at Saints Faith, Hope, and Charity Parish in Winnetka, just north of Chicago. As usual, I took the opportunity to preach about Arrupe College. The gospel reading that day was Luke 5:1–11, which has been an important passage to me for several years now, reminding me that God meets us where we are. It's the one where Jesus meets Peter, James, and John where they are fishing but find their nets empty. Jesus requests that they lower their nets once again, and their nets become so full they are about to burst.

This image of full nets guided—or in keeping with nautical imagery, anchored—my tertianship experience in 2009 and 2010, as I completed the final phase of my Jesuit formation. At that time I was looking ahead to completing my term as Loyola School's president in Manhattan. I was uncertain about what would be next but had the sense that God had in store for me another experience of very full nets. I felt as though those nets had been full where my tenure was defined by three things: honoring the past, building community, and professionalizing the culture.

I thought that my nets would be full when, after tertianship, I moved on to the University of San Francisco (USF), a very good move for me in many ways. USF was the site of my transition from secondary education administration to higher education. While leaving New York, where I had worked for thirty years, was difficult, San Francisco seems to be everyone's favorite city. It was a place I really liked and still like very much. And yet I was only at USF for three years before responding to an unexpected call to try again for full nets somewhere else, when I answered the call by Mike Garanzini to serve as the founding dean of Arrupe College.

PART 2

Serving the Greatest Need

Making Higher Education
Achievable, Accessible, Affordable

Innovation

Some alumni of Jesuit higher education institutions recall be-
ing assigned as essential reading John Henry Newman's The
Idea of a University, *but how many get to see the idea of a*
university come to life?
—DIANE FILBIN, ARRUPE COLLEGE BOARD MEMBER

The story of Arrupe College is part of a forty-five year trajectory of Jesuit education in the United States. The story
begins with Nativity Mission Center and School on Manhattan's
Lower East Side, a story that is near and dear to my heart because, as I wrote earlier, I worked at the school in the 1980s and
was a member of the team that began a Nativity school in the
1990s in Harlem. But the Nativity model for educating middle
school students began in the 1970s, when laypeople and Jesuits
started Nativity Mission Center and School to serve boys, mostly
Puerto Rican, living in the projects and in the tenements of the
Lower East Side. This began a movement of middle schools. A
second Nativity school opened in Boston in the 1980s, and now
there are over fifty of these Nativity schools, a network called
Nativity Miguel. The Christian Brothers of De La Salle have also
started their own versions of Nativity schools. Not all Nativity
schools are sponsored by the Jesuits or the Christian Brothers,
but they all share the goal of addressing the needs of students
from low-income backgrounds who don't want to settle for
underperforming schools in their neighborhoods.

In the 1990s the first Cristo Rey High School opened in Chicago. In its innovative model, students work most commonly in corporate settings one day a week to offset their tuition expenses and take courses during an extended day and year schedule for the other four days per week. The Gates and Cassin Foundations provided the initial funding to create a network that now has a membership of thirty-two schools around the country.

Now with Arrupe College the Jesuits are reinventing education again, this time in higher education. While the twenty-eight Jesuit colleges and universities in the United States are deservedly recognized as some of the most effective institutions of higher education in this country, there is also awareness that the tuition at most Jesuit colleges and universities excludes many. In October 2013, then–Jesuit superior general of the Society of Jesus, Adolfo Nicolás, attended a historic, first-of-its-kind meeting of the presidents and board chairs of the Association of Jesuit Colleges and Universities (AJCU) member institutions in Chicago. Fr. Nicolás was very complimentary about the extraordinary work in Jesuit higher education in the United States, but he expressed concern that our post-secondary institutions were becoming too elite and needed to focus on including those who could not afford to attend a Jesuit college or university. This discussion, by the way, occurred a block away from the building that now houses Arrupe College.

Jesuit Mike Garanzini, at the time Loyola University's president as well as Fr. General's assistant for the intellectual apostolate, was present at this meeting. Mike was a transformational leader at Loyola University and a recognized thought leader in the city of Chicago and beyond. Throughout his presidency Mike talked and listened to the presidents and principals, administrators, and college placement counselors of Chicago's Catholic high schools, charter high schools, and public high schools.

One educational leader with whom Mike engaged was Preston Kendall, one of the founders of the Cristo Rey movement and currently the president of the Cristo Rey St. Martin College Prep high school in Waukegan as well as an Arrupe College board member. Preston recalled:

Mike and I were both guests at a dinner party when Mike asked how things were going at Cristo Rey St. Martin College Prep, where I had recently taken the reins. I bragged that our graduating class of just fifty students had garnered over ten million dollars in financial aid offers from colleges. Mike responded with a question that cut me to the quick: "How much of the ten million dollars was offered to students in the lower half of the senior class?" I stammered, saying I suspected less than 20 percent was offered to those students. Mike nodded, "That's what I thought. What are we doing for those students?"

We talked about many related issues. Job growth over the last several years has greatly favored positions requiring college degrees. Unemployment rates are consistently lower for individuals with degrees. Earnings over a lifetime are overwhelmingly higher for those with college degrees than for those without. Family income is still the most accurate predictor of the quality and quantity of education a person receives. The cost to attend college has vastly outpaced inflation, so many individuals from low-income families cannot afford it. The majority of those from low-income families are persons of color; racial diversity on college campuses does not accurately reflect the diversity of our citizenry, and representation of low-income students is disproportionately lower. There is a widening gulf in the United States between wealthy and poor, and a rapidly shrinking middle class. Community colleges graduate less than 25 percent of all students that start associate's degree programs, and the percentages drop to single digits for African American males and Latinos.

Based on his own vision and fueled by Fr. General Adolfo Nicolás's concerns and his conversations with educators like Preston Kendall, Mike came up with the notion that the Jesuits should create a special college that would offer a high-quality two-year degree program at a very low cost specifically designed for students who have the capacity to go to college but who need extra support.

To make the financial model work, Loyola University would have to cover a lot of the overhead, and all of the students would have to qualify for Pell Grants and for state aid, which in Illinois is called the Monetary Award Program (MAP). With those financial resources, students would be billed less than two thousand dollars a year, which, of course, is a tremendous opportunity.

Preston recalled some of the early discussions:

College is very expensive; let's make our model affordable. Often students don't get good advice on selecting appropriate courses toward a degree; let's give them active and involved advisers. Low-income students do not have extensive support mechanisms to weather stress, bad luck, or other unfortunate occurrences; let's have extra counseling and direct access to social workers when needed. Commuter students often do not feel a connection to their school or classmates; let's create a welcoming space and social activities.

About our project at Arrupe, Preston says, "I believe Arrupe College has the potential to change the face of higher education."

What the Nativity model did for middle school education, what Cristo Rey brought to secondary education—can it happen in our colleges and universities?

Right City, Right University, Right Time

How could I not say yes to being part of such an exciting and necessary project?

—Preston Kendall,
Arrupe College board member

Have you ever had the feeling that your timing was just right? For Arrupe College to begin at Loyola University in Chicago at this time in the history of higher education in the United States feels like that: the timing is just right.

Chicago has been the locus of many important Jesuit initiatives that have gone national. In addition to the Cristo Rey network, they include the Ignatian Volunteer Corps for retired people to share their gifts through service agencies that directly serve those in need; the Ignatian Spirituality Project, which works to end the injustice of homelessness by offering retreats for those on the road to recovery and a better life; and Charis Ministries for young adults. These programs are evidence of a spirit of innovation and opportunity in Chicago, one that was immediately clear when I moved to the city and met with many different stakeholders of the Loyola University community, particularly faculty and staff, who enthusiastically embraced Mike Garanzini's vision of starting this new kind of Jesuit college.

Loyola University Chicago has the capacity to start this project and make it a success. In this early phase of Arrupe College the two greatest gifts for Arrupe are Loyola's brand and infrastructure.

On the issue of brand, we knew from the beginning that very few people outside the world of Jesuits or Ignatian spirituality know the name Arrupe. We're educating our students about who Fr. Arrupe was, but for those who didn't go to a Jesuit school and learn what an important part of Jesuit educational ideals Arrupe was, the name is a mystery.

It's worth noting here that our namesake, Jesuit Fr. Pedro Arrupe, led the worldwide Society of Jesus during very tumultuous times, from 1965 until 1983, when he had a stroke; he died in 1991. Much loved by the Jesuits and the world, Fr. Arrupe was a deeply spiritual man who spoke the truth in love. In the 1970s he delivered a very courageous talk to alumni from Jesuit colleges and universities—big shots, many of whom were big donors (they were all male, as most Jesuit schools at that time were all male). In so many words, he told them: "I'm glad that you're professionally successful and financially successful and I'm glad that you're writing checks to your alma maters, but if you are not men for others, particularly those at the peripheries and the margins, then we really failed you. Because our expectation is that you take your training and your talent and put it at the service of those who have not benefitted from the training that you've received in Jesuit schools." This became the clarion call of the Jesuits in educational endeavors. Now anyone who has gone to a Jesuit high school, college, or university in the last thirty years knows the whole point of Jesuit education is to become "men and women for others." Father Arrupe's spirit is alive and well in the mission of our new school.

While the Arrupe brand is being developed, everyone in Chicago knows the Loyola brand. So the Loyola brand gives Arrupe College instant credibility, as does our location. By moving the business school out of Maguire Hall to new quarters across the street, Loyola gave us a prime location at 1 East Pearson, on the southeast corner of Pearson and State, just a block away from the El stop at Chicago and State.

Beyond giving us a brand and a building, Loyola University Chicago also has the financial capacity to absorb what eventually will be four hundred students without placing a burden on other students or on the staff and services at the school. More than four hundred students and the larger university would not be in ideal position to make it all work.

The city of Chicago is also primed for an Arrupe College. The five most important cities in the United States, in my opinion, are Chicago, Los Angeles, New York, San Francisco, and Washington DC. I think it's fair to say that right now Chicago is the most vulnerable of those cities. When I arrived, I was blown away by Chicago's unfunded pension crisis. The city's pension debt is more than double that of the next city that faces this issue, New York, which is more than three times Chicago's population. In terms of overall debt Chicago is not far behind Detroit, which recently went through bankruptcy.

Then there's the violence. For New Yorkers, the number 343 is meaningful—that is the number of firefighters who died at the World Trade Center on September 11, 2001. I'm afraid that 762 reflects another tragedy; 762 homicides occurred in Chicago in 2016. The violence combined with the debt and corruption of elected officials has caused Chicago to lose population. The same is happening throughout Illinois; in 2016 Illinois lost more residents than any other state. There's talk of Chicago being overtaken by Houston as the third largest city in the United States, and Pennsylvania taking over the position of the fifth most populous state in the Union.

Recently our district's Illinois state representative, Ken Dunkin, visited Arrupe. Ken is in his early forties, African American, and very charismatic. I gathered six of our students to meet with him, and he bedazzled them with his charm and eloquence. I was less charmed, because during Ken's visit I was fretting about the budget impasse in Illinois and the fact that

Illinois state aid, the "MAP money," had not been appropriated yet by politicians in Springfield, the state's capital. During our first year of operation, more than 2,000 students at Loyola were affected, and 110 of those students were Arrupe College students. So, I said to Representative Dunkin, "Look, save the sizzle; I need steak. And the steak is for the folks in Springfield to figure out the budget, release the MAP funding, and do the right thing."

Recently someone asked me somewhat sarcastically, "Aren't you glad that you moved to Chicago at this time?" I was in New York in the 1980s and early 1990s when the crime rates were high there, when people were shaking their heads about the state of things in a city many perceived to be in decline. Of course, since then, New York has gained a reputation as the safest large city in the country, if not the world. In Chicago, it's a different story. But I responded positively, "Chicago is a great city and was good to me long ago when I came here as a young Jesuit to study philosophy. But most important, forget about me, it's about these students and Jesuits going to where the needs are greatest."

What are some of those needs? In Chicago's city colleges, only 7 percent of students graduate in two years. Academic advising for those city college students is almost nonexistent. And in Chicago, only 57 percent of African American males graduate from high school.

I am honored to be part of a team that is attempting to begin to address those needs. The challenges seem overwhelming—but maybe that is why this is the right time for Arrupe College. And if we can make this new model work in Chicago, why can't it be replicated at other Catholic, Jesuit, or secular colleges and universities all around the country?

Helping Students Cross the Finish Line

I remember the many aspirations that were invested in me by not only my father but also the rest of my family. I wanted to become a role model for my younger relatives and end the perpetual cycle of lack of education that had burdened my family for far too long.

—ARRUPE STUDENT

On a Sunday in late February 2016 friends of mine, Jay Morton and Mike Phillips, invited me over for breakfast at their home near Arrupe College. Before I headed over, I read an article in the *New York Times* by Susan Dynarski, a professor of public policy, education, and economics at the University of Michigan, whose work on higher education is very pertinent to what we are trying to accomplish at Arrupe College. In that particular Sunday morning article, "How to Help More College Students Graduate," Dynarski describes how students between the ages of twenty-two and twenty-seven who graduated with a bachelor's degree are earning $43,000 on average, while those who completed only high school are earning $25,000 on average. Over the course of a lifetime, college-educated people earn more those whose education stopped at high school many times over. Dynarski continues to describe the challenges and stresses that first-generation college students face.

Almost all of our students at Arrupe are the first in their families to attend college. Dynarski writes that for first-generation students it's an incredible achievement that they even enroll in college in the first place. For those who do, she says, 30 percent of first-generation freshmen drop out of school within three years, which is three times the college dropout rate of students whose parents went to college.

What fascinated me about Dynarski's findings is that there is no single reason why the dropout rate of first-generation college students is so high. Dynarski explains that often first-generation college students have less money, are less academically prepared to be successful in college, and have fewer resources overall. But a major contributing factor is that first-generation college students don't have parents who can offer them the advice, support, and voice of experience that college-educated parents can provide their children. While great high school teachers, mentors, and guidance counselors are vital, Dynarski explains that it makes a real difference for young people to be able to have both casual and serious conversations with parents about the importance of education and advice about things such as balancing courses and workload, especially when juggling a part-time job.

When I arrived at Jay and Mike's home, another good friend, George Hamel, was visiting on his way to a football game at his alma mater, University of Wisconsin–Madison. I got to know George and his wife, Pam, when I lived in San Francisco; Pam is vice-chair of the board at USF. They have been extraordinarily generous donors at Arrupe College. It was wonderful to see them all and to talk about Arrupe and the article I had just read.

Jay tutors at Arrupe. Early in our first year he was working with a young man named Vincent, a great young person with an endearing personality. That said, Vincent is extremely unfocused. Jay felt frustrated when Vincent would forget to bring his books and assignments or forget about appointments.

During our visit we talked about the challenges Vincent faced being a first-generation student, and how Dynarski's article pertained to him and other Arrupe students. Jay could be available three days a week to work with Vincent, but Vincent hadn't passed any of his classes. His grades improved slightly, but if he didn't pass, the chance of him persisting at Arrupe was unlikely.

We try to keep an intense focus on our students who are struggling, assisted by many friends and supporters of the school who ask how they can help. "Tutoring," I always respond. So these volunteers tutor students, but not just on an academic level. They are, as Pope Francis would say, *accompanying* our students. It's in those casual conversations, as Susan Dynarski indicated in her article, that students learn about navigating college and life. To use a startling image, there's a sense in which the students who are not responding to the services at Arrupe College need to be "ambushed." Jay, for example, had to wait at the door as Vincent walked out of the classroom.

We've invested in these students. We have made a commitment to them and to watch them flounder and fail is unacceptable. I'm very concerned about making sure that we fulfill our promise of helping students across the finish line to graduation—a key metric by which we measure success at Arrupe College.

Achievable, Accessible, Affordable

I chose to come to Arrupe College for a few important reasons, such as its affordability and credibility, class size, and the fact that it is part of Loyola University. I am one of those students who learn faster in a small environment, and when I went to the interview for admission I was told that the class size would be small. This really grabbed me because it meant that I would get the attention I need to be successful. And money wise this was perfect. I could have gone to other schools and just taken out so many loans, but Arrupe was different. I would be graduating with a degree and no debt.

—ARRUPE STUDENT

Everywhere you look at Arrupe College, from our hallways to our mission statement to our promotional literature, you'll find the same phrase: *achievable, accessible, and affordable.*

Let me say a word about this tagline. In September 2014, when we were preparing for Arrupe's launch, we wanted the school to be known for its access, its affordability, its accountability, and its achievement. Loyola University's talented marketing and communications team helped develop the idea of using those four attributes as a tagline or brand. I really liked three of the A's—*achievable, accessible, affordable*—but *accountable* didn't sit well with me. It sounded like we were already confronting what were then hypothetical students about hypothetical deficits. I didn't want to start that way. I'm all about accountability and so is Arrupe College, but it didn't need to appear in our tagline.

Now that the first three have been established as the tagline, there's a danger in glossing over what each word means and the challenges we face to make higher education achievable, accessible, and affordable.

Being from New York and having worked in education there as a Jesuit, I'm struck by the fact that only 9 percent of those enrolled in the city's two-year colleges graduate in two years. National averages are even lower—only 5 percent of those enrolled in two-year colleges graduate in two years. In Chicago, the numbers seem to be better: 17 percent of those enrolled in two-year colleges graduate in two years. But in a talk I recently attended by Cheryl Hyman, the chancellor of the City Colleges of Chicago who is resigning after six years at the helm of a troubled educational system, she said that the graduation statistics do include certificate programs. The 17 percent graduation rate may not reflect an "apples to apples" comparison with the graduation rate of other two-year college programs. When certificate programs are not included, the graduation rate is likely to be closer to 7 percent.

One of the most staggering statistics in Chicago is that a student in one of the city colleges meets with an adviser only once during enrollment. There are heartbreaking stories about students who register for classes without being advised and find out later that they're out of sequence or have other obstacles to graduating on time or at all.

So, to make higher education achievable, accessible, and affordable, we focus our energies on our location, how we construct our classes, and how we accompany our students each step of the way.

Statistically, 60 percent of our incoming freshman class, Arrupe's class of 2018, self-identifies as Latino, 31 percent African American, 5 percent biracial, 2 percent white, 1 percent Asian, and 1 percent Native American. Fifty-four percent of our students come to us from Chicago public high schools, 23 percent from Chicago charter schools, and 23 percent from Chicago Catholic schools. All are fresh out of high school—these students are just coming off their proms and graduations—and that is by design. We want to have relationships with feeder schools. We want to have relationships with college placement counselors who can say "he's worth the risk" or "I'm concerned about her."

Our inaugural class, the class of 2017, was 70 percent Latino and 21 percent African American, and people wondered why our statistics didn't match Chicago's ethnic makeup—roughly, one-third black, one-third Hispanic, one-third white and Asian. Part of the reason is that Arrupe is a Spanish name, and we are a Catholic college, so there's an affinity among the Latino community. Recruitment for the class of 2018 targeted high schools that report very high African American enrollments. Consequently, we have a higher black enrollment for the freshmen.

We recruit students with an expected family contribution (EFC) of less than $5,234. The cost for an Arrupe education is $12,328, but because the students commute, because Loyola is leveraging the fixed costs of the building we share with the

School of Social Work, because we fundraise, and because all of our students who are citizens complete the Free Application for Federal Student Aid (FAFSA), we are able to bring the cost per student under two thousand dollars a year. When people say that Pope Francis is the best current Catholic story, I say Arrupe's affordability is a close second.

Here are some more numbers. The goal at Arrupe College is eventually to enroll two hundred students in the freshman year and two hundred in sophomore year. The local PBS channel recently reported that the Chicago city colleges announced a drop of 25,000 students since 2012, but they still have an enrollment of 113,000 students at their seven campuses. So why is our goal only two hundred freshmen, when the need is so great in Chicago? Part of it is capacity—we only have three floors available on our campus at the current time. In addition, our students deserve Arrupe's "high touch" culture, and "high touch" would be more difficult to achieve with high enrollments.

During orientation for our administration, faculty, and staff, I make a point of telling them that in addition to their primary jobs, their role at Arrupe is to be advisers for our students. This is something that really gets the attention of anyone who cares about what we are doing at Arrupe, especially our existing and potential benefactors. Metrics matter, so we track everything—where is the student in terms of her GPA? How did he do on his midterm exam? Did she turn in that paper? His mother was just deported, so does he need housing and help? These are not imaginary scenarios; they are very real, and they can surface at any time. I tell our team that advising students is a huge part of their work, and I hope that it is also the most satisfying. By gaining multiple perspectives about our students, our team is able to help them stay in school and graduate. As time goes on, this type of accompaniment also helps our team know what to look for when interviewing potential students to assess their grit, perseverance, and resilience.

The other piece I emphasize with our team is that we are changing the game for Jesuit higher education and higher education in general. Congressman Robert "Bob" Dold, US Representative for Illinois's 10th Congressional district (Chicago's North Shore) met with a group of our students in the spring of 2016. He asked them an easy question, "What's been your favorite class so far?" A struggling student named Rhonda gave an answer that I think surprised the congressman. "I like philosophy. You know, reading Plato and Aristotle and Augustine and Aquinas and learning how they think has really influenced the way that I think."

My hope, I tell our team, is that what we're doing at Arrupe influences the way the Jesuits and the world think about how to deliver higher education, especially to young people like Rhonda and our other students.

Beyond the Benchmarks: Relying on God's Grace

In November my father died. When I returned to Arrupe after three weeks I was welcomed and I started getting back to work—everything was arranged so that I could catch up. I had new deadlines for finals and assignments and my teachers were really caring. From there I started working my way up, and I couldn't believe that I passed all my classes. I was proud and grateful to God because without Him, I could not have made it and without Him, there would have been no Arrupe and amazing faculty and staff to help me go through it all.
—Arrupe student

I celetrate mass on Saturdays or Sundays with the people of Saints Faith, Hope, and Charity Parish in Winnetka, thanks to my fellow Loyola University dean and fellow Jesuit Tom Regan, who introduced me to pastor Fr. Marty O'Donovan shortly after I moved to Chicago. The parishioners hear a lot about Arrupe College, mainly because I see our students and their situations when I pray and prepare my homilies for mass. I'm grateful to the Faith Hope community. Despite my reservations that they may be hearing too much about Arrupe, the feedback I receive is positive. "How's the college, Father?" they ask if I don't preach about Arrupe.

On July 3, 2016, I presided and preached for the Fourteenth Sunday in Ordinary Time. I focused on Luke 10:1–12, 17–20, in which Jesus missions seventy-two followers to go ahead of him to proclaim the good news, and Galatians 6:14–18, admonishing believers not to boast but to rely on the grace of God.

Meditating on these readings gave me pause.

But first, a quick aside. I'm very driven by quantitative data. As dean of Arrupe College, a big part of my job is tracking numbers, statistics, metrics, and benchmarks. Board members, benefactors, foundations, and Loyola University are very interested in our numbers. So, for example, I can tell you that on the Fourteenth Sunday of Ordinary Time in 2016 our students had an average GPA of 2.66, an increase from 2.55. We had twenty-three students in each class. Our budget for the fiscal year was $5.3 million, including the cost of a capital project. Of that, $3.1 million came from Pell and MAP Grants. In the middle of July I was anticipating orientation for our incoming students. That costs $639 per student.

More numbers: Our breakfast and lunch program costs $1,000 per student. We give our freshmen computers that cost $650 each. For our rising sophomores, our college transfer counselor will offer them college tours, looking at schools in Illinois, Minnesota, Indiana, Wisconsin, and Missouri. That's going to cost $800.

Yet more numbers: Given the dismal graduation rate of city colleges locally and nationally, I am following and emphasizing our freshman and sophomore retention rate. We started with 159 students in August 2015; almost a year later our enrollment was 143. In July we had retained 90 percent of our original student body.

Fr. Jim Keenan, a good friend of mine who is an outstanding ethicist at Boston College (BC) and was one of my theology professors at Weston Jesuit School of Theology (now part of BC), visited in May. When I told him that we have a 90 percent retention rate he exclaimed, "That is the same freshman/sophomore retention as Boston College!"

There was only one appropriate response from me: "Well, I hope and pray that the students at Boston College can keep up with those at Arrupe College!"

Back to the Sunday readings. They reminded me not to put my focus on metrics and any boasting that may come from them. Paul in Galatians says that it's not about boasting (he could be talking to contemporary US culture). Rather than focus on being self-reliant, he says, realize your dependence on the grace and favor of God. Luke recounts that as the seventy-two disciples went out to the towns, they could have focused on numbers and stats and metrics—how many healings, how many exorcisms, how many people preached to. But Jesus reminds us that triumphalism is an inappropriate spirit among the disciples. Luke tempers enthusiasm for mission success with insistence on a more enduring gift: to have one's name inscribed on the roster of the citizens of heaven.

Another Loyola University Chicago Jesuit, Fr. Jack Kilgallen, helped me to understand how we need to remain grounded in Jesus by pointing out that in that gospel reading, whatever astounding things the disciples do, or whatever wise things they say, none of that substitutes for Jesus himself. This is a good reminder of the servant role of disciples. This is a good reminder that every healing and preaching cannot take the place of Jesus. This is a good reminder to me that the quantitative successes cannot take the place of Jesus. This is the Jesus who sends the disciples out in pairs so they model mutual support and a living embodiment of the gospel of peace.

At Arrupe College the associate dean for academics, Jennie Boyle, and I pair up regularly to meet with students who are struggling. In addition to our desire to help these students, I am also aware that a major dip in enrollment will cause our funding sources to ask what happened. So I am driven by the stats; yet, in our encounters with the students we face so many life events that simply are not quantifiable.

During one such meeting Jennie and I spoke with Carlos, whose grades tanked because his best friend was shot and killed. Carlos explained that nothing like this had ever happened to him and that he was a little distracted. No kidding. Why wouldn't he be?

We met with Donnell and LaDonna, both of whom are homeless and are overwhelmed with their life situations. We met with Eduardo, who missed a full week of school to caddy at a country club because his mother had no money coming in. As the oldest child with no father at home, he had to lug as many golf bags as he could to make the rent payment and support his mother and siblings. Jennie and I met with Rhonda, the philosophy enthusiast, who was embarrassed to tell us that she has no Internet connection at home. She was trying to do her homework on her smart phone. She is scared to go out at night to find Internet access, and there is no Starbucks in her neighborhood.

We met with Teresa, whose mother was deported recently. Teresa is caring for her nine-year-old sister, who is despondent without their mother. Teresa admits that she herself is experiencing depression. Of course she is.

Listening to these students put the numbers in perspective. The life stories behind them came to the fore. The metrics melted, and the benchmarks became secondary. The students' stories of suffering and sacrifice and strength took precedence over the statistics.

The experience called to mind *Angela's Ashes*, the great memoir by Frank McCourt about an Irish family living in poverty in Limerick. One vignette has remained with me. Young Frankie is the oldest of the family, and his father is an alcoholic; his mother has just had another baby, and his father has taken the baby's formula money to the bar. Eight-year-old Frankie goes to the bars looking for his father, hunting his father down for the money for his mother and the baby. Frankie is also starving, and at one of the bars he doesn't find his father but he does find a half-eaten sandwich on the bar. Frankie takes a couple of bites out of it.

Because he's Irish and this is the 1930s, Frankie knows that he has committed a sin, and so he immediately goes to confession. When Frankie confesses that he has stolen by taking a bite of a sandwich at the bar, the priest, speaking from a place of great clerical privilege, asks, "Why don't you go home and have your mother fix you dinner?" Frankie explains to the priest: "Father, there's no money at home. Mother has had a new baby; my father is a drinker and he's taken the money to the bars; and we're all starving at home."

The priest, listening to this in the confessional box, pauses and says, "You know, I'm in here every day doling out penances and what I ought to be doing is getting on my hands and knees, washing the feet of the poor." Now this doesn't resonate with Frankie—he's there for penance because he's committed a sin, so he asks the priest, the confessor, "Father, what's my penance?" And the priest says, "There's no penance." Frankie insists, "Look, I came here for penance." The priest pauses again and says, "For your penance, please pray for me."

Frankie not having anything to eat at home is, for me, not unlike Eduardo's inability to go to class because he has to pay his family's bills or LaDonna's and Donnell's drop in grades due to their experiences of homelessness. Like the priest listening in the confessional, I marvel as I listen, and his desire to wash the feet of the poor helps me to understand my desire to provide opportunities and to learn from Teresa and Rhonda and Carlos and their classmates.

St. Ignatius Loyola, the founder of the Jesuits, is often credited with saying, "Pray as if everything depends on God, work as if everything depends on you." This phrase has helped to drive me in my work, along with numbers and metrics and benchmarks and statistics. But in my musings and in my own prayers I am wondering if this could be reversed. Pray as if everything depends on you; work as if everything depends on God. Our prayer has to be urgent, just as the work at Arrupe College is urgent. Also, this reversal of Ignatius's quotation gives us perhaps a different perspective, Paul's perspective in Galatians, Jesus's perspective in the gospel. We work hard, but ultimately it's not about us; we need to leave the outcomes, the numbers, the statistics, the metrics, and the benchmarks to God. A tall order, grounded in prayer and in acknowledging who Jesus is in our lives.

The gospel that Sunday ended with this admonition from Jesus: "Do not rejoice that the spirits submit to you, but rejoice that your names are written in heaven." We will rejoice when the names of Carlos, Donnell, LaDonna, Eduardo, Rhonda, and Teresa are written on their diplomas from Arrupe College.

PART 3

The School

*Building a New Model
of Jesuit Higher Education*

Hiring for Mission

When I first heard about Arrupe College I was very intrigued.
. . . Being part of the inaugural group of Arrupe faculty has
been an adventure of many new beginnings.
—KATE NISSAN, ARRUPE COLLEGE FACULTY MEMBER

When I began my ministry at Arrupe College in September 2014, the tasks of starting a new two-year college at Loyola University seemed endless. First among them was the need to get approval from the Higher Learning Commission (HLC). Arrupe's status as a college within a well-established and respected post-secondary institution like Loyola University gave us much credibility with the HLC—another reminder of the strength of the Loyola brand. That said, this was the first time a college or institute at Loyola would be awarding a two-year degree; consequently, HLC needed to conduct a review.

Much of the preliminary work for that was orchestrated by members of the Loyola team, but it still had to be brought to execution. A team of educators from other four-year and two-year higher education institutions visited us in January 2015. We were anxious, but I knew it was going well when one of our visitors asked if he could contact me after the visit because he'd like to replicate what we are doing at his own college. Later in the spring there was white smoke over Pearson Street; we had our accreditation.

Before that, though, I had started to hire my colleagues. The first person was my administrative assistant, Wendolyn Gomez.

Wendolyn is a graduate of Cristo Rey Jesuit High School and Loyola University Chicago. St. Ignatius's prayer for generosity could be about Wendolyn, particularly his desire "to give and not to count the cost." Wendolyn is generosity personified. I'm grateful for the positive and professional ways Wendolyn represents Arrupe College and me.

In place already for our admissions work was Derek Brinkley. Derek works for Loyola University and had arrived in Chicago around the same time that I did. He hails from another Jesuit educational institution, Xavier University in Cincinnati, where he also worked in admissions. He works part time for Loyola University and part time for us. He is an admissions professional par excellence.

We needed someone to do admissions full time, so our first admissions director was another Loyola University alumna, someone who was also working already in Loyola's admissions office, Viviann, or Viv, Anguiano. Viv began with us in February 2015, recruiting our first class, setting up our admissions interviews on Sundays beginning in March, and also running numerous information sessions and visiting countless schools. Viv is now earning her master's degree at the Harvard University School of Education. When she told me she was leaving to return to school, I had a hard time protesting; I earned a master's at the same school, and it was the best educational experience I've ever had. I'm happy that she has this opportunity.

In March of 2015, Yolanda Golden joined us as associate dean for student success. That job title is not on Loyola University's human resources list, but I insisted on it. It sent a strong message to Loyola and to the students we were recruiting at that time that we are here for their success. Yolanda worked at Loyola for many years in the School of Social Work. She has a great sense of who our students are and what their needs are. She is very generous with her time, very hard working, and a terrific colleague.

Three more people were recommended to me early on, the first being Dr. Jennifer Boyle. Jennie has a strong background in Jesuit education, having earned her BA from the College of the Holy Cross and her PhD from Loyola University. Provost John Pelissero suggested that Jennie might make a good dean of academics for us. Jennie chaired the political science department at Elmhurst College, a local college in Chicago's western suburbs. I met with her in the fall of 2014.

When I check references, I try to reach out to someone not on the candidate's list. In Jennie's case, that person was Kris Cupillari, dean of students at Loyola School in New York. Kris and Jennie had lived in the same residence hall at Holy Cross, and Kris gave her stamp of approval. I offered Jennie the job. Jennie needed to complete her year at Elmhurst College, so she began working for us part time in April before joining us full time.

Jennie led the charge for hiring our faculty after I hired the first faculty member, Minerva Ahumada, who had a doctorate in philosophy from Loyola University Chicago and was teaching at La Guardia Community College in Queens, New York, one of the largest community colleges in the country. I knew from our first conversation that Minerva understood our students. We were discussing food insecurity, and I asked if that was an experience for her students in Queens. She said that she always brought snacks because she knew that her students had not eaten. The day we spoke on the phone she said she had been tutoring one of her students who seemed kind of woozy and lightheaded. The student explained that she had not eaten in a couple of days, so Minerva shared some grapes with the student. Minerva now teaches philosophy at Arrupe College.

Farrah Ellison-Moore joined our happy band as the career coordinator. Farrah is in charge of assisting our students in creating resumes and preparing for interviews. She supports them in their work situations and also in finding and succeeding in internships.

We needed a development director, and I found the right fit: Maggie Murphy Stockson. Maggie is a New Yorker and a Georgetown University alumna. Maggie was a member of the pioneering team of Cristo Rey High School in Harlem. I was part of the accreditation team for that school and was very impressed with Maggie at that time. She had moved to Chicago because her husband, Gil, was earning his doctorate at Notre Dame. Maggie was working for a not-for-profit in Chicago, and she was able to join us at Arrupe in July 2015.

In August, Isabel Reyes replaced Viv. Isabel brings much warmth and empathy. She herself was an undocumented student and struggled when she first matriculated at Loyola University Chicago. She understands where a lot of our students are coming from. Prior to Arrupe, she worked for Chicago Public Schools (CPS) and brought deep knowledge of schools that could be great feeders.

The leadership team consists of the two associate deans, Jennie Boyle and Yolanda Golden; the two admissions professionals, Derek Brinkley and Isabel Reyes; the assistant dean for development, Maggie Murphy Stockson; and our business manager, Adam Shorter. Adam works in the provost's office, but he has a background in business, and he understands how Loyola works. Adam helps me navigate the university's procedures and is very committed to Arrupe, to our students, and to their success.

Arrupe's budget covers the salaries for everyone except Adam, who is full time in the university's provost office, and Derek, who works for the larger university's admissions efforts. In addition, Maggie is paid by Loyola University's advancement office. These salary savings are significant and demonstrate how Arrupe can keep costs down as a college within Loyola University.

I meet with Wendolyn every morning, and each of the others once a week. While this level of contact is unusual in higher education, I find these meetings provide opportunities for communication and feedback, which are particularly important for a startup. We also meet together for the Dean's Leadership Group, an important part of our work that deserves its own discussion.

The Dean's Leadership Group

Never let a serious crisis go to waste. It's an opportunity to do things you think you could not do before.
—RAHM EMMANUEL

When I was president of Loyola School, I hosted a weekly President's Leadership Group, which consisted of the headmaster (or principal), Jim Lyness; chief financial officer, Susan Conniff; vice president for advancement, Tony Oroszlany; and facilities manager, Maryann Asprea. Although I met with Jim, Susan, Tony, and Maryann individually on a weekly basis, the group gave us the opportunity to interact. It was important, for example, for Tony and Susan to hear of new initiatives Jim was considering for Loyola School students so that Tony could begin to identify donors and Susan could think about financing. If Maryann had a physical plant concern, she communicated it to the members, who in turn passed on the issue to other stakeholders.

At Arrupe College I have a Dean's Leadership Group (DLG), which consists of the two associate deans, Jennie Boyle and Yolanda Golden; the two admissions personnel, Isabel Reyes and Derrick Brinkley; the development director, Maggie Murphy Stockson; and the business manager, Adam Shorter. We meet as a team on Tuesdays at 2:00 p.m., and I create an agenda based in part on their input.

The first DLG met on July 7, 2015. Our orientation for our students was beginning later that week. Jennie spoke on our computer order, because we planned to give all of our students laptops. At that time Viv Anguiano was still our admissions person, so she gave us an update on our admissions numbers, and Adam Shorter did the same on the budget. Funding and logistics for our breakfast-and-lunch program concerned me. All of this was covered during the DLG's maiden voyage.

The following week we talked about Viv's replacement, welcomed Maggie, and had our first media gig, an appearance on Telemundo where two students, Javier and Bianca, ably represented us. We talked about an official ceremony for Arrupe's opening. I updated my colleagues about my first meeting with Beth Purvis, Illinois Secretary of Education, and I also expressed my concern about out "real estate." We have the first three floors of Maguire Hall at Loyola University, and when we first opened it seemed to be ample space. Yet we filled it up quickly, and I wanted to check on our needs for office space and meeting space, as well as our crucial classroom space. Jennie generated a course catalog, which we reviewed for the first time. We recapped our experience with orientation planning, which included a "bravo" for Yolanda Golden, for the orientation leaders, and really for everyone. We also talked about students of concern, anyone that we felt we needed to discuss as a larger group. These topics were wide ranging, and the meetings offered the chance to get everyone's input.

Reviewing the agendas of those first DLGs reminds me of how much we had on our plates in order to get Arrupe up and running. Viv Anguiano transitioned to Harvard, and Isabel Reyes began working with us. Isabel and Derek proposed dates to interview prospective students for the next class. Maggie and I heard from both Walmart and a private family foundation that we had received funding for both the meal program and a retreat program. Yolanda and Farrah were putting together a jobs exchange so that our incoming students could find part-time employment. At the DLG on July 28 we were anticipating the end of the summer enrichment program with our first mass and awards, scheduled for July 31, the Feast of St. Ignatius. We also began to identify a couple of students whom we were concerned about. One did not persist with us. His close friend had been shot that fall, someone he described as like his brother, and he ended up withdrawing. The other student came to us with little preparation for success in college. It was discouraging, almost shocking to us that she had been promoted through elementary, middle, and high school, because she was reading at a fourth-grade level and was profoundly challenged in her processing skills. We knew she would require much attention.

We also discussed how to make our coursework become pathways to employment, particularly for nursing. One of our students, Marlynn, had spoken to Yolanda and me about her desire to become a nurse. She had considered leaving Arrupe College and transferring to one of the City College branches that offered special programs in nursing. She tried to contact my counterpart online at City College, but only a phone number was available; she called and the voicemail box was full. Then she went to the City College branch and was told that she was not college worthy, though it was our understanding that City College's admission is open. Marlynn remained with us; she thrived, actually. I was delighted and honored to sign a letter recently congratulating her for making the dean's list.

Marlynn's experience influenced us. At an August DLG I reported on meetings with a foundation that was very interested in financing the software, the computer lab, and a virtual lab for anatomy and physiology classes for our students who were interested in nursing or pre-nursing. On other fronts, Yolanda was arranging with PNC Bank for a financial literacy class. Loyola University Chicago's School of Education was beginning to document our startup, so two doctoral students attended the

DLG meetings. We began to look at creating another administrative position. While my assistant, Wendolyn, is capable, generous, and smart, all roads were leading to Wendolyn, and my work wasn't getting done.

It was also in August that I first identified the need for a college transfer counselor. What happens to Arrupe students when they graduate with their associate's degree? What's next? We also discussed computer disbursement; through the generosity of Pam and George Hamel, we were able to purchase laptops for all of our students. By August we also realized that our first food service provider did not include a dedicated worker from the caterer to oversee the operation. I felt such a person was important to set a tone and to monitor what was popular. Maggie was on board at this point and was beginning to do outstanding work trying to figure out financial aid and scholarship opportunities with the money that had been raised.

Our first DLG gatherings surfaced two critical takeaways. First, success for Arrupe meant making fundraising a priority. The summer enrichment program; the breakfast-and-lunch program; laptops for the students; scholarships, particularly for undocumented students ineligible for aid—none of these funding needs were anticipated in the initial planning for Arrupe. A commitment to provide these and other services was necessary.

A college transfer counselor was also key. Many of our students wished to transfer to a four-year college, and after their experiences as Arrupe students, they would be well prepared to do so. Our students see themselves as Loyola University students; they develop an affinity with the larger institution. Loyola, a fiscally healthy university, does not have the capacity to absorb scores of juniors accustomed to paying less than two thousand dollars a year when Loyola's tuition is over forty thousand dollars a year. Consequently, a college transfer counselor was needed to assist students identify other four-year options, find the most robust financial packages, and complete the myriad forms in order to transfer.

My reflections about those early DLG meetings brings to mind the goal St. Ignatius set for all Jesuits—to be contemplatives in action. The Arrupe faculty and staff had the "action" part down as we welcomed and enrolled our first class. The "contemplation" engages me now, helps me make sense of our priorities, and also guides me when I speak with peers from other post-secondary institutions when they discuss their interests and desires to start their own versions of Arrupe.

The action undertaken by the members of the DLG at the end of August included planning the formal dedication of Arrupe College. Chicago Archbishop Blase Cupich and Mayor Emmanuel were to be present and speak, as were State's Attorney Anita Alvarez and interim and former presidents John Pelissero and Mike Garanzini, SJ.

On the financial aid side Maggie began meeting with students to inform them that they had received scholarships and who their donors were (and to remind them to write thank you notes to them!). Maggie also took on the responsibility of our website, which we discussed during DLG as well.

Another topic of discussion that September was Loyola University's large Jesuit community, including many young Jesuits fresh out of the novitiate. They've taken their vows, but before they go on to teaching or other ministries and then on for formal theology studies on the path to ordination, they do first studies, usually a combination of philosophy and theology. It's a real blessing to benefit from the goodness and energy of these twenty-something and thirty-something Jesuits at Loyola. And, of course, there has been a lot of enthusiasm from the Jesuit community for Arrupe. So three Jesuits scholastics, Nick Albin, Danny Gustafson, and Eric Immel, began volunteering for us during that first September.

At one of our September DLGs, Yolanda Golden recapped the job exchange that she and our jobs coordinator, Farrah Ellison-Moore had put together. Representatives from the Lincoln Park Zoo, a big employer for our students, said that they were very impressed with the organization of the job exchange and also very impressed by our students. Employment is a constant issue for us. We eventually got our student employment rate up to 64 percent by April. A lot of those jobs were in retail and fast food, quick and easy jobs for some of our students, particularly those who are undocumented, who have so much against them in the employment arena. We want our students to see themselves in professional, corporate, or white-collar settings as well as retail and food service. Just as we want them to feel like they belong in higher education, we also want them to grow in their confidence as they consider their career options.

We also talked about Fall Observances—what we might plan for the Feast of All Saints, for Thanksgiving, for the end of the semester. Obviously our identity is Catholic, and we considered it important to recognize visible markers of Catholic faith, but we also wanted to remain aware of the needs and perceptions of our students who are not Catholic or not Christian.

It was around this time of year that a student named Jennifer first appeared on the DLG agenda. Jennifer was a mother of a child with special needs, and she had some learning differences herself. She was, as many of our students are, a commuter with a long commute. She was from a very traditional, patriarchal family, so the expectation for Jennifer was that, because she needed to care for her child, going to college was "nice to do," but not "need to do," and there was not much support for her. We made sure to remember her as a student of concern to help her succeed at Arrupe.

By the middle of September we were negotiating with the Ignatian Volunteer Corps for a volunteer. The Ignatian Volunteer

Corps comprises folks my age and older who work two days a week, and from the very beginning we had a tremendous volunteer response from them. We also discussed the work we needed to do on our tutoring and writing centers, both of which were provided by Loyola University. Our students tend to avoid participating in these centers. For them, going to a tutoring or writing center is an experience of shame. It confirms that they don't have what it takes to be successful in a private Jesuit liberal arts institution. Needing a tutor means, for them, that they don't belong.

As September came to a close, we focused on the grand opening. Andy Lubetkin, our instructor for oral communication, had identified one of his students, Sierra, as someone who would be a very good public speaker, and he was right. Andy worked with her for hours on end to prepare her. I met with her once or twice. She was nervous, but her best delivery, of course, was on the day of the grand opening. She was the star of the show.

It was an honor to have Mayor Emmanuel and Archbishop Cupich present, and after Sierra spoke about how much she loves statistics and how much she loves numbers, Mayor Emmanuel quipped, "If you love numbers so much, how about if you help me figure out the budget?" That was a magical day. Room 110, on the first floor of Maguire Hall, serves as our main gathering space at Arrupe. It was packed with friends of Arrupe College, colleagues from across the university, and our students. When I spoke, I mentioned the famous Pedro Arrupe line, "Fall in love, stay in love; it will decide everything." It is the line I always use to encourage our students to fall in love with the idea that they will be successful college students at Arrupe College. Mike Garanzini and John Pelissero spoke graciously about their high hopes for the students.

Archbishop Cupich talked about how fortunate the students are to know Jesuits. Mike Garanzini and I weren't expecting these remarks, and it was simultaneously very elevating and very humbling. The great affection for the Society of Jesus the archbishop feels was palpable.

Mayor Emmanuel also did a nice job. I had previously met him at an event during his reelection campaign. When I recruited him for our opening (to be fair, it was one of our board members, Susana Mendoza, the city clerk, who really delivered on this), I reached out to him by reminding him of our previous encounter. And so the mayor attended and spoke. Even better, he lingered after the event and interacted with all of our students. There's a beautiful picture of Yolanda Golden walking Philip, a shy student, over to Mayor Emmanuel; the mayor showered all sorts of attention on Philip. It remains my favorite picture of the year.

When I left full-time teaching for full-time administration, faculty friends admonished me for going over to "the dark side." I don't see it that way. The experience of the DLG in the first months of Arrupe reinforced my vocation as an administrator. There is nothing more satisfying for me than to be a part of a group whose members complement one another with varied and versatile backgrounds and talents that combine to move the organization forward.

Board Formation

Our decision to join Arrupe's board was not a difficult one when I and my fellow board members considered the alternative of standing by and doing nothing in the face of our city's and country's challenges. As Dr. Martin Luther King, Jr., once stated, "The ultimate measure of a man is not where he stands in moments of comfort and convenience, but where he stands at times of challenge and controversy."

—Rick Hammond,
Arrupe College board member

I've always been invested in the work of boards of trustees. In addition to my own board service over the years, which currently includes Regis University in Denver and Cristo Rey Jesuit High School in Chicago, I have done extensive research on the role of boards and what makes them successful. As a Jesuit working in Catholic education, my two particular interests are the vital role of lay leaders in the church as outlined in the documents of Vatican II, particularly *Lumen Gentium (Dogmatic Constitution on the Church)*, and best practices for effective boards. In brief, I believe that boards are one of the best manifestations of the council's emphasis on the laity. Christians are baptized as priests, prophets, and leaders; serving on boards of Catholic institutions is a concrete way of exercising the baptismal call for leadership. I studied thirty-four boards of Jesuit high schools for my dissertation at Teacher's College at Columbia University and have continued my research since then. When I directed the Institute for Catholic Education and Leadership at the University of San Francisco, I created a conference for boards of trustees. I've also spoken and led workshops all around the country, most recently with Nativity Miguel Coalition member schools. Boards have been an essential part of my work as a school president and now as a dean.

Because Arrupe is a college within Loyola University, our board is more of an advisory board than one that has fiduciary responsibilities. That said, I respect our board members' time and investment in Arrupe and work with them as I would any other board.

A key factor for our board is diversity. As of February 2016, we had twenty-one board members, including me. I was the only Jesuit on the board. The Association of Governing Boards (AGB) reported that in the United States, the typical higher education board is 30 percent female and 10 percent people of color. At Arrupe, 50 percent of our board members are women and 57 percent are people of color.

When I was building our board as an outsider to Chicago, I brought a few people with me from outside of the area. One such person is Lidia Bastianich. Lidia is a dear friend and a celebrity chef with a very successful cooking show on PBS. She owns and operates several restaurants in the New York City area, as well as Pittsburgh, here in Chicago, and in Kansas City. She and her son, Joe Bastianich, and their partner, Mario Batali, own and operate Eataly, which is an Italian emporium very popular with residents in New York and Chicago and with tourists in both cities. I know Lidia because her daughter Tanya is an alumna of Loyola School, and I'm very close friends with Tanya and her husband, Corrado Manuali.

A little background story. One year when I was president of Loyola School, my responsibilities there prevented me from traveling to be with my family for Thanksgiving. Lidia learned of this and invited me for Thanksgiving dinner. When my mother heard this, she said, "Well, I don't feel too sorry for you!" When Lidia invited me, I said, "I'll help out and make a little Stove Top Stuffing. How about that, Lidia?" She looked at me like I was out of my mind and said, "Don't worry about it, Father. Just come yourself." That was the beginning of our friendship.

Lidia is really quite remarkable and very entrepreneurial. Eatalys have opened in the World Trade Center and in Boston, the restaurants are thriving, viewers watch Lidia's Emmy award–winning show religiously, and she travels around the world to appear at or provide for delicious fundraisers. Around the time we were starting Arrupe College, she was visiting Chicago to check in on her Eataly operations, so I popped the question: "Lidia," I said, "I am involved in arguably the most entrepreneurial activity in Jesuit higher education, and you're an entrepreneur, so I need you on this board." Lidia was predisposed to saying yes. She responded, "I knew this question was coming. I've had children who've gone to Boston College and Georgetown University after attending Fordham Prep and Loyola School, and now I have grandchildren at Boston College, at Regis High School, and at Fordham Prep. They talk about Jesuit spirituality and discernment, so I wanted to discern and pray about this decision of joining the board." She continued, "When I pray, I pray to Holy Mary, Mother of God. So, I prayed, 'Holy Mary, Mother of God, Father Katsouros is going to ask me to join his board. What should I do?'" Lidia reported that the Mother of God said to her, "You do whatever Fr. Katsouros asks you to do." (Whenever I can be on the same side as the Mother of God, that's a good thing for me, and it's a great thing for Arrupe College.)

Another board member not from Chicago who has been a great resource for Arrupe is Mark Shriver. Mark presented at one of the trustees' conferences that I hosted in San Francisco, and he did a superb job; he's a terrific speaker. When I first asked Mark to join the board, he told me to forget it. "No way, Katsouros," was his response. I said, "Yes, Mark, you are going to join this board." Mark shook his head, called me "relentless," and has been an ongoing asset for our work.

I credit my mother for Mark's membership. When I was nagging him to join the board, Mark was experiencing some back trouble; in fact, we were at a CVS drugstore looking for heating pads and other remedies when my mother called me on my cell phone. My mother is a member of the Rosary Society where she lives, and she, my aunt, and other older Irish Catholic women gather on Tuesday nights to say the Rosary. So I said to my mother, "Look, I'm with Mark Shriver, and his back is bothering him. Mark and I want to know if the Rosary Society would pray for his back?" "Of course," she said. A few weeks later Mark called me, and I asked how his back was. He said, "Your mother is a miracleworker. My back is great. Now tell her that my knee is kind of out of whack. Can the Rosary Society pray for that?" So later that day my mother called, and I told her that I had been on the phone with Mark Shriver. She asked, "How's his back?" So I said, "Nice going, Ma, his back is fine. Now it's his knee. Can your prayer warriors say the Rosary for his knee?" My mother paused and then asked, "Does this guy have any health insurance? Why is he relying on a bunch of old women saying the Rosary for his medical needs?" That has remained a great joke between Mark and me, and in both our families.

Mark's family includes Peace Corps founder Sargent Shriver and Special Olympics founder Eunice Kennedy Shriver. Mark runs Save the Children Action Network. He is a great advocate for young people, in particular for pre-K education, and, as a graduate of Georgetown Prep and the College of the Holy Cross, is an enthusiastic supporter of all things Jesuit. Mark has been passionate about our work and has also introduced me to several graduates of Holy Cross who live and work in Chicago. Two of his classmates also joined Arrupe's board.

Mark has generously shared his contacts because he understands networks. One of the things I emphasize heavily with our board is the importance of networks in helping young people to succeed, something Robert Putnam explores in his book *Our Kids.* Our students and their families do not come from or benefit from the same networks as we do, or as so many of other students who attend Jesuit schools do. I remind the board that I rely on them and their networks to benefit our students and Arrupe College.

Some examples: One of Mark Shriver's classmates who serves on our board is Sean O'Scannlain. As president and CEO of Fortune Fish, the largest food distributor in the Midwest, Sean was invaluable as I was shopping for a meal program for our students. Similarly, Adela Cepeda is in finance here in Chicago, and she's been very helpful in identifying who in Chicago would be a promoter for Arrupe. She's also providing a job for our students. Diane Filbin works at BMO Harris, one of the local banks. BMO Harris provides financial literacy workshops for our students. Anita Alvarez, the first female and first Hispanic to serve as state's attorney for Cook County, Illinois (2008–2016), was instrumental in connecting me with the group 100 Black Men, which assists African American high school students applying to college. When 100 Black Men met in October 2015, our admission officers, Derek Brinkley and Isabel Reyes, and I staffed a booth at one of their events at the University of Illinois at Chicago. Anita also attended the event and took turns with us at our booth talking with young black men about the opportunities at Arrupe College.

Preston Kendall, one of the founding fathers of the original Cristo Rey Jesuit High School in the Pilsen neighborhood of Chicago and president of one of the newer Cristo Rey schools, St. Martin College Prep in Waukegan, introduced me to B. J. Cassin, whose foundation has been very supportive of the Cristo Rey network.

Our board chair, Joe Seminetta, is an alum of Loyola University Chicago and, as one of our board members observed, a self-made man. As luck would have it, Joe is also a parishioner at Saints Faith, Hope and Charity Church where I preside on Sundays. It's been a blessing to get to know Joe and his wife, Denise, and their three sons through their faith lives in our parish as well as through our collaboration at Arrupe College.

This past February, Joe and I gathered with an ad hoc group of board members—Rick Hammond, Stephanie Chapman, Luis Gutierrez, and Adrianna Tulman—to work on one of the iterations of our mission statement. After the meeting I was able to talk about the financial contributions of our board members. Following my experience at Loyola School, I mandate that every board member has to make at least a five-figure contribution each year. This request came as a surprise here at Loyola Chicago when I first specified this obligation. Someone who wanted to be on the board said to me, "But I have so many ideas for you." I responded, "I went to Harvard and Columbia. I'm good with ideas. Arrupe needs cash." As St. Ignatius would say, "Deeds, not words." Rick and his wife, Donna, sponsor five Arrupe students who need financial assistance. Stephanie is the assistant dean of Loyola University's School of Social Work and brings a practitioner's perspective as well as long experience as an administrator at Loyola. Luis works in finance and is deeply committed to the ideals and spirituality of the Society of Jesus and to our students. Adrianna gathered her friends to form a junior board for Arrupe—twenty- and thirty-year-olds who aren't able to give five figures—yet—but can help with interviewing, tutoring, and smaller fundraisers.

Another of our board members is Bill Lynch, who is one of the presidents at Wintrust, a bank here in Chicago that has a very strong presence in the life of the city. Bill has been very supportive of Arrupe College and has had Wintrust underwrite the catering at our admissions events. I told Bill that the caterer had two price points for the bar. A Marquette University graduate, Bill looked at me in astonishment and reminded me of my vocation. "Father, you're a Jesuit. Top shelf." Bill has opened his rolodex, and his colleagues at Wintrust have introduced Arrupe to several civic and business leaders and influencers.

I met Gieriet Sullivan Bowen through her Holy Cross classmate Mark Shriver. Fun, energetic, and thoughtful, Gieriet worships at Saints Faith, Hope, and Charity with her family. She and her husband, Ted Bowen, had heard me preach about Arrupe College and were very enthusiastic about our mission. When I asked Gieriet to think about joining the board, she said she had previously served as a trustee at Holy Cross and that she'd consider my invitation. One weekend after mass I suggested that it might help her discernment if she visited Arrupe. The next day Gieriet attended an admissions event at Arrupe for prospective students and family members. Gieriet asked the candidates, "Why are you applying to this school? What's in it for you at Arrupe College? Why does this interest you?"

Gieriet reported that no matter if the students were male or female, African American or Latino, the responses were all the same: they wanted to find a way to go to college without burdening their families. Moreover, they spoke about a college degree as a path to help their parents and their siblings down the road. Gieriet was wowed by our students, by their altruism, by their focus on others. That sealed the deal. At the end of the event she turned to me and said, "All right. I'm in."

Arrupe College is blessed with an engaged and prudent board. I love the collaboration that happens among its members and through them, through their networks and their generosity toward Arrupe College and their support of me. I really do see *Lumen Gentium*, with its focus on the holiness of laypeople, alive in our board. Just as Vatican II emphasized, they are called by virtue of their baptism to exercise leadership in Catholic apostolates like Arrupe College.

Crafting
Our Mission Statement

Only by being a man or woman for others does one become fully human.

—PEDRO ARRUPE

On Friday, January 29, 2016, members of the Arrupe College community and I gathered to work on Arrupe's mission statement. Given all of the other more pressing matters related to getting Arrupe College off the ground, we hadn't found the time to craft one yet. I invited a diverse group to be part of the in-house committee: Osmar Cruz, first president of our student government; Asya Meadows, another member of our student government; Farrah Ellison-Moore, our career coordinator;

Minerva Ahumada, our philosophy professor; and Wendolyn Gomez, my administrative assistant.

In preparation for our gathering I sent the group some helpful resources. The first was a document on the difference between a vision statement and a mission statement that was developed by R. J. Valentino. R. J. runs a consulting group in California called the Napa Group and was my coach when I was president of Loyola School. The second was the address that Jennie Boyle, our associate dean for academic affairs, delivered at our academic convocation on January 27. Jennie gave an impassioned talk to our students that emphasized four values: excellence, justice, compassion, and collaboration. I also included Loyola University's mission statement; our student government's mission statement; a document that Maggie Murphy Stockson, our development director, put together for Arrupe's advisory board and our junior board; and a helpful document from Board Source called "What Is a Mission Statement." It took us about an hour to come up with a statement. Quite frankly, I had expected it to take longer.

The group agreed that we needed to emphasize our Jesuit identity and Fr. Arrupe's vision of forming persons for others. We also agreed that the four values Jennie highlighted in her address should appear in our mission statement. The consensus was that we also needed to include the three A's we use in all of our promotional materials: *achievable, accessible,* and *affordable.* Finally, I argued that we needed to include the term *liberal arts.*

To this last point, I was influenced by Scott Carlson's article in the January 22 issue of the *Chronicle of Higher Education* about our student demographic and the kinds of jobs that they think about for themselves. Carlson wrote that for students from low-income backgrounds, the kinds of careers that they think about for themselves have to do with survival. Students from more affluent backgrounds think about careers that have to do with their self-determination and are more aspirational. Students from low-income backgrounds are often not counseled to pursue the liberal arts because they need jobs and they need education that is more job focused. This well-intentioned advice, however, can limit the advisee's trajectory. The research indicates that a liberal arts background leads to higher-paying jobs and allows for more versatility for the graduates. So I wanted to include "liberal arts" in the mission statement.

At the end of our hour together, this is what we had agreed upon:

> As Loyola's two-year college, we embody the call of Jesuit leader, Fr. Pedro Arrupe, to be persons for others. In a collaborative and compassionate way, we strive for excellence and work for justice by providing a rigorous, innovative, liberal arts, Jesuit education that is achievable, accessible, and affordable.

Done in two sentences! I was delighted.

Of course, there were still questions—Is *embody* the right verb for the first sentence? Should we say, "In collaborative and compassionate ways," or should we say, "We strive collaboratively and compassionately for excellence"? But that second sentence fulfills the role of a mission statement, and the first sentence is somewhat visionary and aspirational and grounds us in the Jesuits, in Pedro Arrupe, and in being persons for others. The bottom line for me was that we crafted our mission statement without much influence from me. It was important for our students, faculty, and staff to identify Arrupe College with the person of Fr. Pedro Arrupe, with being a Jesuit institution, with the Jesuit ideal of persons for others. I was also very pleased with how Jennie's four values influenced this work. I brought Jennie into my conference room afterward, where we had the draft of the mission statement posted on my wall, and I think it was very affirming for her. I was happy that her contribution and her remarks from two days before had so deeply influenced our work.

After that first meeting Arrupe board chair Joe Seminetta and I hosted two gatherings of board members to assist in the mission statement exercise. Kelly Shannon, Loyola University's vice president for marketing and communication, and Jesuit author Jim Martin also took turns at wordsmithing.

At Arrupe College's spring board meeting, Joe Seminetta rolled out the following:

> Arrupe College is a two-year college of Loyola University Chicago that continues the Jesuit tradition of offering a rigorous liberal arts education to a diverse population, many of whom are the first in their family to pursue higher education.
>
> Using an innovative model that ensures affordability while providing care for the whole person—intellectually, morally, and spiritually—Arrupe prepares its graduates to continue on to a bachelor's program or move into meaningful employment. Heeding the call of its namesake, renowned Jesuit leader Pedro Arrupe, SJ, the college inspires its students to strive for excellence, work for justice, and become "persons for others."

Admittedly, this is much longer than our first mission statement composed by the internal committee six weeks before. That said, our faculty had embraced it—writing instructor Sean O'Brien uses the iterations of Arrupe's mission statement to illustrate the power and process of revision. Osmar, Asya, and the rest of the student body also expressed enthusiasm. At the board meeting, when Joe completed his reading of the mission statement, he called for a vote of approval from the board. Unanimous. Applause followed.

I often emphasize that the word *mission* comes from the Latin verb *mittere,* which means "to send." So what is our mission? What are we sent to do or to be? We are sent to be persons for others, to strive for excellence, to work for justice, and to provide this rigorous, liberal arts, Jesuit education. We have a mission. We know why we were sent here.

Student Interviews

When I was a senior in high school I spent the majority of the year focused on attending another university, and when I didn't get in, I was crushed. Originally, coming to Arrupe destroyed my spirit; it made me feel as if I had missed a great opportunity. But this was a lie. Arrupe was my opportunity.
— ARRUPE STUDENT

On January 23, 2016, we conducted our first interview day for our next incoming class, the class of 2018. Interviewing our applicants was Mike Garanzini's outstanding idea. All of our students apply online and include their transcripts and an essay, but what distinguishes the most serious applicants is their willingness to travel to Arrupe College for an interview.

Our faculty and staff served as interviewers, along with colleagues from around the university—women and men, faculty, administrators, staff members, particularly people of color—and Loyola alumni as well. The interview process created a lot of good will and good buzz about Arrupe. Before the interviews began, I told our volunteer interviewers, "You're really influencing this new initiative by participating in these interviews, and you're also influencing the lives of young people from around Chicago."

I found these interviews moving. You see students come in, hope filled. We designed the interview to help them reveal their best and to help us assess their grit, persistence, and resilience. We asked students to describe an obstacle or setback—sadly, many of them are all too familiar with obstacles or setbacks. We paid attention to how they handled adversity, what they learned from it, whether they sought help, and how they might have received help.

During the interviews Yolanda Golden, our associate dean for student success, shared with me that she'd witnessed two of our volunteer interviewers from our inaugural class, Jody and Isaiah, going above and beyond to welcome the applicants, particularly the ones who seemed to be nervous about their interviews. Yolanda observed that our two students spent a lot of time calming the students, encouraging them, and assuring them that the interviews would go well. I was impressed with their leadership and grateful for their help in setting the right tone and making a great first impression on the applicants for the next class at Arrupe.

One of the applicants, Julio, was accompanied by his father. Julio was all dressed up. He was very earnest and very assertive. Julio explained to me that he was undocumented and was concerned because he was ineligible for Pell or MAP grants, which cover tuition for most of our students. Back in November, our development director, Maggie Murphy Stockson, and I had met with Don Graham in Washington DC. Don is the former publisher of the *Washington Post*. He has directed his considerable energy toward TheDream.US, an advocacy group based in Northern Virginia that creates opportunities for young people like Julio to go to college. Last winter I forged a relationship with TheDream.US president Candy Marshall, and we agreed that Arrupe College would be a partner school with TheDream. US. Undocumented students enrolling in partner schools can receive funds to make up for what they aren't receiving in federal and state aid.

I asked Julio if he'd heard about TheDream.US, and he said yes. So I said, "Fill out an application. If you need help with that, see Isabel Reyes. Isabel is our director of admissions and will get you through the process." Just looking at Julio and his father, I could see that they are *sencillo*—very simple in a most beautiful way. Arrupe is the ticket for Julio, for his father, for the rest of his family, and for their futures. It is frustrating to me that a young man of promise like Julio is denied access to the ten thousand dollars from Pell and MAP grants that make an Arrupe College experience available and accessible to his peers.

We had so many prospective students register for interviews that we needed eight more interviewers. I asked for help in an email to all of the Jesuits who are members of the Loyola University community. Young scholastics responded to the call. So did Fr. Jack O'Callaghan, a great Jesuit in his eighties who has been a leader on a national and international level with the Society of Jesus. I was touched by my Jesuit brothers' enthusiasm and support for Arrupe College, their encouragement to me, and their presence on interview days. It made concrete the enthusiasm and encouragement and support I've felt from the Jesuits about what we are attempting to do for Jesuit higher education at Arrupe.

When we have admissions events, I talk about Fr. Pedro Arrupe to our prospective students and any family members or counselors from their high schools, so they know where the name of Arrupe College came from. I base my presentation on a powerful quotation often attributed to Arrupe:

> Nothing is more practical than
> finding God, than

falling in love
in a quite absolute final way.
What you are in love with,
what seizes your imagination, will affect every-
    thing.
It will decide
what will get you out of bed in the morning,
what you do with your evenings,
how you spend your weekends,
what you read, whom you know,
what breaks your heart,
what amazes you with joy and gratitude.
Fall in love, stay in love,
and it will decide everything.

After my best stab at a dramatic reading, I apply Arrupe's words to our candidates. I say: "While you're here you may fall in love with one another, but that's not a big priority for me; rather, I want you to fall in love with the idea of being a college student. I want you to fall in love with the idea that you can be a successful college student in a Jesuit, liberal arts college, here on the Gold Coast of Chicago, called Arrupe College at Loyola University Chicago." And I assure them that if that happens, it will affect everything.

I say, "I hope that a professor or a staff member or a course will seize your imagination, whether it's Western Civilization or stats or philosophy. What gets you out of bed in the morning will be your desire to be at Arrupe to attend classes, to build community with us, and to advance in your education. What you do with your evenings, well, you can anticipate a lot of work, a lot of studying, perhaps group study, as well as writing papers and rewriting papers and engaging in the life of being a freshman and sophomore in college. How will you spend your weekends? Well, it could be the same thing. Hopefully there are some social aspects as well. In addition, we work with all of our students in terms of job placement, so a lot of time on the weekends could be spent working and developing professional skills."

I go on, "What you read—Descartes and Junot Díaz, Toni Morrison and Ernest Hemingway, theologian James Cone and playwright Zora Neale Hurston—will shape you. Who you meet—classmates, young women and young men from various parts of Chicagoland, our faculty and staff, and the larger Loyola community—will widen your circles and your experiences. What breaks your heart—there are going to be some obstacles along the way and maybe some events that are larger than just obstacles—will make you stronger and more compassionate."

I conclude, "We will be filled with joy and gratitude if at the end of two years we are celebrating you and your achievements, if you are receiving an associate's degree from Arrupe College at Loyola University Chicago, if you have earned your degree and incurred little to no debt. So, if you fall in love with this idea of being a college student with us for the next two years, it will decide everything."

I find it heartening to hear our current students talking about how they have fallen in love with statistics or theology or philosophy. How they've fallen in love with seeing themselves as college students. How they have fallen in love with seeing themselves as academically successful. How they have fallen in love with their growth in confidence. How they've fallen in love with their desire to pursue a four-year degree, a master's degree, a doctorate. So this transformation, this falling in love that affects everything, that decides everything, as Fr. Arrupe says, we are seeing borne out in our students.

Summer Enrichment Program

The purpose of the Summer Enrichment Program is threefold: (1) to provide a foundation for students that transitions them from high school to college by developing content that focuses on the executive functioning skills needed for success in a collegiate setting; (2) to place students in their cohorts and provide opportunities for community bonding, networking, and group identity formation prior to their first semester of classes; and (3) to introduce students to the values of Arrupe and the university as it relates to Jesuit traditions and beliefs.

—YOLANDA GOLDEN, ARRUPE COLLEGE,
ASSOCIATE DEAN FOR STUDENT SUCCESS

We take our Summer Enrichment Program (SEP) very seriously at Arrupe College. The program includes three weeks at our building at Loyola University's Water Tower Campus, plus a weekend at the Loyola University Retreat and Ecology Center (LUREC) in Woodstock, Illinois. It's not rocket science, but all of the research indicates that student success and retention rates increase if students attend an orientation where they meet future classmates and faculty members; learn a little bit about the lay of the land, such as where their classes will be held and how to get to the college or university; and—here's the key—register for classes under the guidance of an academic adviser.

Arrupe's associate dean for student success, Yolanda Golden, directs SEP. She emphasizes the importance of the incoming freshmen's experience at LUREC. By removing the students from their comfort zones and bringing them to LUREC, they immediately have to assume care for themselves away from their families. This places more responsibilities on them and supports the message that they are now competent and capable adult learners who are in control of their academic and behavioral outcomes. Yolanda recalls one student's experience. "I have never been away from my parents before, and it was really scary for me to come to LUREC. I almost didn't choose Arrupe because of this, but I am glad that I did. I met friends when I thought I wouldn't, and I learned I could make decisions on my own and still be okay." Yolanda trains student orientation leaders to guide the incoming freshmen through skits that cover a range of topics from substance use to community building.

At the Water Tower campus the orientation continues. There, Yolanda says, "students engage in rigorous classroom sessions with Arrupe faculty and campus partners designed to foster their group work skills and resiliency in problem-solving new experiences. Throughout SEP, students focus on time management, fiscal responsibility, honoring commitments, professionalism, and critical thinking as they explore topics related to philosophy, theology, career development, and networking with peers, staff, and faculty."

Let me share a story to illustrate how important SEP is and what a turning point it can be for students.

Last summer a member of our inaugural class, Jante, was really enjoying SEP. A very personable young man, who had graduated from a Chicago charter school, Jante was sailing through orientation. He liked his classmates, our professors, and the entire Arrupe College experience. But Jante had a dilemma. During the second week he approached me and said, "Fr. Katsouros, my mother wants to take me on a trip to Las Vegas. I would miss four days during the last week of orientation, Monday through Thursday." We are insistent about the importance of attending the entire SEP; we tell the students that they can't miss orientation or they will jeopardize their enrollment at Arrupe.

So, I responded, "Jante, to paraphrase an old expression, 'if you go to Vegas, then stay in Vegas.'" He was dismayed. I said,

"Look, I can't make an exception for you." He pursued this, and I said, "Jante, go for the weekend, and I'll look the other way if you aren't here on Monday, but you have to return Monday night and be here on Tuesday." I really thought that I would not see Jante again, and that wore on me because he is a great young man and we thought Arrupe would be such a terrific fit for him.

Monday morning arrived at SEP, and so did Jante. "What happened to Vegas?" I asked. He answered, "I decided not to go." I was impressed. I said, "Jante, you have made a great decision. I know that I'm not your favorite person right now. I know that your mother is probably not going to invite me over to your house any time soon for dinner, but I don't care. What I care about is that you chose long-term gain over a short-term thrill." I shook his hand. "Jante, congratulations, wise decision."

Six months later at our academic convocation, at the end of the program, I presented our first Spirit Award to the student who best exemplifies the spirit of Arrupe. The recipient was Jante. He now works in our admissions office and is an outstanding tour guide. Yolanda observes, "He speaks to prospective students regarding the importance of making their education a priority, even when it may be inconvenient." Jante speaks from experience—his experience of good decision making during the SEP.

We Are Happy to Serve You: The Breakfast and Lunch Program

Enjoy life with great food and friends.

—Lidia Bastianich,
Arrupe College board member

My father, Nick Katsouros, died in November 2014. I was blessed to have visited with him and my mother just weeks before his death in their home in a development in suburban Maryland called Leisure World. They really enjoyed living there and formed a good community characterized by strong, supportive friendships.

When I last saw my father, he was very interested in what we were doing in Chicago. He was solicitous and concerned about the high crime rates in the city. He was also happy that there is a Greek Town in Chicago featuring many Greek restaurants. My father was a restaurant owner. He operated a diner called Nick's Grill. His diner featured a neon sign that flashed "Steaks," "Chops," "Steaks," "Chops," endlessly. The staff was wonderfully diverse. The cooks in the kitchen were Anna and Mr. Deodes, as well as my grandfather and various other Greek family members and friends, whipping up everything from spanakopita to baklava. Working the floor was the wait staff, four African American women: Bertha, Hilda, Pat, and Daisy. Bertha was a churchgoing, God-fearing woman. I can remember my mother giving Bertha a lot of her hats once the Catholic Church no longer required women to cover their heads to attend mass. For Bertha to worship at her AME Baptist Church without a hat was unheard of. Hilda was quiet and hard working. Daisy had a big personality. Pat wore a huge button on her waitress uniform that read, "Tipping is not a city in China"—very subtle. The janitor was a diligent, loyal fellow named Grover.

The clientele were people from all walks of life in DC: white-collar professionals, tradesmen, electricians, plumbers, police officers, people associated with the federal government, and neighborhood residents, African American families, teenagers, young mothers pushing strollers, old people pushing walkers. In other words, the kingdom of God.

Customers patronized Nick's Grill because of my father's warm hospitality—and because of the great food. As a high school student I suspected my popularity with my peers was based on the fact that I was the pathway to Nick's Grill. We would descend on the restaurant for burgers or fries or sandwiches, and to this day I've never found a restaurant with better shakes than those my father made.

I believe the first sentence that I could sound out was, "We are happy to serve you"; it was emblazoned across all of the coffee cups at Nick's Grill and so many other diners owned and operated by Greeks. Decades later, when I worked at Loyola School in Manhattan, I would tell that story about my father's diner and say to families whose children were applying to Loyola School that same phrase: "We are happy to serve you."

Because of what my father did for a living, meals have always been important to me. He was always gracious, concerned about or focused on food and whether customers had enough to eat, and if they enjoyed the meal and if he could get them anything else. My father was service personified. A simple guy whose education ended when he received his high school diploma, Nick was a man for others long before Pedro Arrupe coined the phrase.

Before we launched Arrupe College, I was beginning to think we might need a meal program, an incentive to come to school. I was aware that our students would be coming to us from high schools where they qualified for free or reduced-price breakfasts and lunch, and I was also aware that hunger doesn't end at the age of eighteen. This came up in a conversation that I had with one of our board members, former Atlanta Falcon football player Earl Jones. Over lunch one afternoon he described how he coached young men in football in Austin, a neighborhood in Chicago. Earl stated that these young athletes were hungry. Naively I asked, "You mean hungry for competition? Hungry for victory? Hungry to improve their athletic skills?" Earl looked at me, shook his head, and said, "Father, they're hungry for food." It all came together. My conversation with Earl happened around the time that my father died. And so it became a bit of a personal mission for me to get a breakfast-and-lunch program going.

Another key conversation transpired a few months later with Dan Cardinali, the former president of Communities in Schools—the largest dropout prevention group in the country—and now president and CEO of the advocacy organization Independent Sector. Dan and I connected in February 2015 and discussed a meal program at Arrupe. He directed me to the Walmart Foundation, which has supported our breakfast-and-lunch program with gifts totaling over $200,000.

Additionally, a graduate of Loyola University, Mike Sullivan, has given $100,000 to support the program, and Billy Miller, whom I've known since he was in high school at Regis High School (we worked together later at Nativity) and his wife, Sara, provided us with another $50,000. Later they teamed up with Lidia Bastianich for a fundraiser in their home to provide our students with nutritious daily meals.

The original food service I hired was fine, but it just dropped the food off; it did not provide a server. That's not how it would have been in Nick's Grill; it seemed impersonal to me. In November of our first year, I reached out to board member Sean O'Scannlain for help. We vetted other food services together, and eventually we found a terrific food company called HandCut.

HandCut began working with us in January 2016. A wonderful woman serves our meals and knows our students. The menu is nutritious, and much is produced locally, as HandCut subscribes to the farm-to-table movement.

I try to eat with the students when I can. In *Our Kids* author Robert Putnam describes the importance of family meals, especially in an era when family dinners are on the decline. Putnam cites research showing that high school graduation rates increase and college matriculation rates increase because parents are spending time with their children at dinner. I'm trying to simulate that atmosphere at Arrupe to some degree. I love talking to our students about their classes.

One day one of our students, Dennis, raved about the sweet potatoes, so of course I had to sample them. Another afternoon HandCut served tacos, which led to a conversation about the best Mexican food in Chicago. I look forward to following up on the students' recommendations.

Important things happen over meals. For Catholics, the sacrament of the Eucharist is based on gathering around the table and breaking bread together. My father knew the importance of meals at Nick's Grill, where there was a unique and vital community. We are also building community at Arrupe, and breaking bread enhances the experience.

I don't know how students can sit in classes, study, and take tests in statistics and theology and Western civilization and math on empty stomachs. Our breakfast-and-lunch program provides them with two healthy meals a day, and it also provides us with an opportunity to build community. My father's influence is very much alive at Arrupe. We are happy to serve you.

Serving Undocumented Students

My mother once told me that she was afraid I would break down at the moment of realization that despite my hard work at high school, this country does not offer me the same opportunities as a US citizen. I am an undocumented student, but my faith and hope reside with God, and I remember replying to my mother, "The Lord will provide. Don't worry, I am going to college."

—ARRUPE STUDENT

At the end of June 2016, I was reading the *New York Times,* as I do most mornings, and came across an article that hit close to home about the Supreme Court decision in *United States v. Texas.* The article explained that the justices had deadlocked in a case challenging President Obama's immigration plan, a sharp blow to an ambitious program that Obama had hoped would become part of his legacy. As a result, as many as five million immigrants would not be shielded from deportation or would not be allowed to work legally in the United States. The four-four deadlock left in place an appeals court ruling blocking the plan, thus amplifying the already contentious election-year debate over the nation's immigration policy and presidential power. The case concerned an executive action by the president to allow unauthorized immigrants who are the parents of citizens or of lawful permanent residents to apply for a program that would spare them from deportation and provide them with work permits.

The program was called Deferred Action for Parents of Americans and Lawful Permanent Residents (DAPA). I know one of those parents. Her daughter, Teresa, is a student at Arrupe College. Teresa is one of over sixty students enrolled at Arrupe who is undocumented. The percentage of undocumented students enrolled at Chicago area state schools is generally 3 percent or lower. A local Catholic college claims 10 percent of its students are undocumented. At Arrupe College, 20 percent of the students identify as undocumented.

At the end of June, Teresa told me that her mother had traveled to Mexico after having lived in Chicago for over twenty years in order to "fix her papers." Teresa explained that everything was going well with her mother's visa process until the judge asked about her daughters. Teresa's mother answered honestly that the oldest of her four children was born in Mexico and was six months old when the family moved to America.

According to Teresa, the court denied her mother reentry to the United States and charged her with human trafficking for traveling with her infant daughter. The family began working with lawyers to petition for the mother's release and return but knew that several months could pass before the family would be reunited. Teresa reported that she had become very depressed and that her younger sister, nine years old, was despondent.

In light of the 2016 election and Donald Trump's campaign promise to build a wall to keep out Mexicans, whom he has called rapists and criminals and terrorists, we are compelled to advocate for Arrupe College students who are undocumented or who are the children of undocumented parents. Teresa's situation is unfortunately a very familiar one to all of us at Arrupe.

To help Teresa, I wrote a letter on her behalf for her lawyer:

To whom it may concern:

I am Rev. Stephen Katsouros, SJ, a Roman Catholic priest and a member of the Society of Jesus (the Jesuits). I am dean and executive director of Arrupe College at Loyola University Chicago. I am writing on behalf of Arrupe student Teresa M____. I have known Teresa for over a year. We met when she was applying for admission to Arrupe. Teresa is an impressive student and an important member of our college community. Her transition from high school to college has been successful as of this writing. Teresa's GPA is 3.29. She contributes positively to our community. She participated in our college's first theatrical production last spring. When I wished to consult with students about undertaking a capital project at Arrupe, I solicited advice from Teresa because I trust her judgment and intelligence. She is a positive influence among her peers and is respected by my colleagues and me. She is well positioned to complete her two-year degree in two years, and I am confident that she has the capacity to transfer to a competitive four-year college or university and experience success there. Her mother's situation could easily upend Teresa's progress and success. She has spoken with my colleagues and me about her concerns. I am most impressed with Teresa's care for her younger sibling who is grieving her mother's absence. I worry about the toll that this situation is taking on Teresa and her entire family.

Teresa completed her summer courses at Arrupe about a month after the Supreme Court decision. Before the fall semester began, she traveled with her little sister to see their mother, now living in a detention center. I wondered if they would return. They did. Her mother is still in Mexico. Teresa had learned the lyrics to *Hamilton* and could break into a rendition of "The Battle of Yorktown" with some of her classmates at the drop of a hat last year. She still has a light touch about her and enjoys many friendships at Arrupe, but she is noticeably distracted. A friend who is an immigration attorney has taken on Teresa's case on a pro bono basis, but it is one among tens of thousands in Chicago. The waiting continues.

I check in with Teresa. "You know, Father," she confided recently. "I suffer from depression." Why wouldn't she?

Fundraising

I am thankful to receive this scholarship. It has made a great impact on my college experience because it gives me hope as an African American young woman that there are people who care about my future.

—ARRUPE STUDENT

"I could never ask them for that."

That was the response from a president of a university when I told him I expected board members to give at least a five-figure contribution each year to the institution they were governing, and he should too.

"Look at it this way," I responded. "By asking them at that level, you're saying two things. First, you're saying, 'I think you have been so successful professionally or so prudent with your resources that you have the capacity to give at this level.'"

"What's the second thing?" the president asked skeptically.

"You're saying, 'Your values, who you are, your family, what you hold dear all align with, mirror, are on the same page with the mission of our institution—a mission that is so important, so valuable, so necessary.' Either way, you're complimenting the prospective donor."

Henri Nouwen eloquently summarizes this relationship in his monograph *The Spirituality of Fundraising* when he writes, "Asking people for money is giving them the opportunity to put their resources at the disposal of advancing the Reign of God."

Fundraising was not anticipated when Loyola planned Arrupe College. Mike Garanzini and the advancement team at Loyola secured a one million dollar gift from the McCormick Foundation, to be paid out over three years. The gift, from one of the most respected and established foundations in the country, indicated that Arrupe was worthy of investment.

I will always be grateful for the generous support provided by our friends at the McCormick Foundation. But it wasn't enough. Undocumented students, scholarships, laptops, emergency hardship cases, the summer enrichment program, visits to colleges—the list of needs goes on.

My life as a fundraiser began in 1991 during my regency in Harlem. At that point many of my contemporaries outside of the Jesuits were beginning to experience professional success and were also beginning to think about philanthropy. On Friday nights, over a drink and dinner, friends would ask about my school, my students, Harlem. Soon, the stories would accumulate, and someone would say, "All right, Steve, I'll pay for his books," or, "How much is tuition?" or, the fundraiser's preference, "Steve, here's a check. It's unrestricted. Use it for whatever you think is the greatest need."

There wasn't a plan for fundraising at Arrupe after the extraordinary McCormick Foundation gift, but the stories of our students, their talents, and our aspirations for them abound. Two close friends of mine on the West Coast have given over a half million dollars because they recognize Arrupe's important mission. Wintrust Bank in Chicago has pledged a half million dollars through the leadership of board member and Wintrust president Bill Lynch. Other board members and friends have given at the six-figure level.

Much of our success can be attributed to Maggie Murphy Stockson. She is the ideal fundraiser—she knows the students, interacts with them regularly and meaningfully, can represent our needs to donors and foundations with authenticity, and offers a macro perspective while paying attention to the details. She is prudent, pastoral, and a good steward of our donations.

Both Maggie and I are focused on building a donor base of Chicagoans. Several of our donors gave to Arrupe when my father died and my family posted the "in lieu of flowers" notice in his obituary, as did friends from previous chapters of my life who knew my father and wanted to support Arrupe. Others are friends from both coasts who are enthusiastic about our work. We don't have a typical donor base; we have no alumni. Foundations like McCormick are enthusiastic and responsive, but foundations often provide seed money for startups and then move on to support new ventures. Consequently, we are determined to establish an annual fund populated primarily by Chicagoans. Arrupe College exists for young residents of Chicago.

When Maggie and I meet with donors or pitch our cause, we are careful not to present our students as a demographic of deficits. Arrupe College has needs. That said, Arrupe is attracting remarkable, talented, and tenacious young people. Yes, Arrupe provides our students with a unique opportunity. Arrupe also provides Jesuit higher education with an opportunity—to learn and benefit from our students, their stories, and their achievements.

I discussed this with one of our students, Magdalena. Her perspective informs mine. "Often I have found people around me pushing me to ask for pity because I am an undocumented and poor brown woman," said Magdalena. "Those who pushed me to ask around for pity tried to help me but instead created insecurities. About 90 percent of my high school classmates— including myself—were low-income and Hispanic. My high school always mentioned those sorts of details but forgot to mention how bright some of the students were." Magdalena concluded, "I do understand pity can influence donors into digging into their pockets, but why have people feel sorry for us when we can impress them instead?"

The word about impressive students like Magdalena and their accomplishments at Arrupe is getting out there, through our board, through Loyola's publications, through the university's alumni, through education circles consisting of people concerned about what happens after high school. Chicagoans love their city and embrace Arrupe when they meet and listen to Magdalena and her classmates.

One gift from a Chicagoan is quite memorable. Maggie stopped in my office with an envelope addressed to me. One of our freshmen had dropped it off when I was attending a meeting. It was our first Christmas season at Arrupe, a time when mail is especially meaningful for advancement personnel because many donors make end-of-year gifts. I opened the card. It was from the student's grandmother, who wrote,

"Hoping that every day of the New Year finds you in good times, good health, good cheer, God Bless, Gertie." Inside the card were two five-dollar bills—the widow's mite (Luke 21:1–4). I carry Gertie's card with me as a reminder that of all the gifts we have received at Arrupe, the greatest gift is to see how God is active at Arrupe and how much I have to learn from our community.

A Scholarly Community and a Rolling Boil

I can proudly say that Arrupe has shaped who I am today. Being part of student government, among other things, has brought me much more confidence and appreciation of others. My social skills have consistently improved, and I keep growing as a person. Arrupe College is more than I expected. A student only needs a will to grow and improve to succeed at Arrupe. I could not be more thankful to God and Arrupe College.

—Arrupe student

Each morning I walk through Maguire Hall to interact with students on my way to my third-floor office. When I ask, "What's happening at Arrupe for you today?" I receive a range of answers.

"I'm nervous about my presentation in oral communication, Father."

"We're watching *Inglorious Basterds* in ethics class."

"Big test in macroeconomics—pray for us, Father."

"I'm revising my paper about gangs and gun violence for writing and composition."

"We're discussing *Titus Andronicus* in Shakespeare class."

"Regression analysis in statistics—didn't you call that class 'sadistics,' Father?" (I did. I shared with our students my struggles in statistics during my studies at Teachers College.)

Arrupe offers three associate degree options: arts and humanities, social and behavioral science, and business. When students complete their two years, they will have earned sixty-one credits—thirty-seven hours of general education core requirements, fifteen hours of pre-major concentration classes or electives, and nine hours of Arrupe College mission-related core requirements—that are fully transferable to most Illinois institutions and many out-of-state colleges and universities as well. Mission-related core requirements include courses in theology, religious studies, ethics, and philosophy.

Each student takes four courses per semester and two courses in the summer for two years for a total of sixty-one credits including a lab course. Each course meets twice a week. Students attend Arrupe for three hours on Monday, Tuesday, Thursday, and Friday as members of either the morning or the afternoon cohort.

I presumed the afternoon cohort would be heavily subscribed. I projected my memories of being an undergrad, which included sleeping late in the residence hall where I lived.

Arrupe students, however, gravitate to the morning cohort. They are accustomed to going to school in the morning, as they did during their high school years. In addition, several students are uncomfortable returning to their neighborhoods after dark.

The academic mission is led by associate dean Jennie Boyle. "The opportunity to participate in creating a college that would respond to the urgent need to create greater access to higher education and would operate according to the principles of *cura personalis* was incredibly compelling for me." Jennie continued, "The first year has been a whirlwind of activity on the academic side of the house, and I have enjoyed (mostly) every minute. By far the consistent highlight of leadership is engaging with faculty who have a shared, passionate commitment to serving the students. . . . We are aligned in creating a scholarly community that operates according to the values of compassion, accountability, transparency, and striving for excellence."

Seeking excellence, *magis* in Jesuit-speak, drives Jennie, the faculty, and staff, as does the notion of *cura personalis*. English instructor Sean O'Brien explains: "*Cura personalis* is a concept that I've always believed in as an educator, even before I learned the Jesuits' unique articulation of it. It's also something that I've grown into more over the course of my first year at Arrupe."

Cura personalis is advanced by our instructors, who also serve as advisers. For me, this is the key characteristic at Arrupe. Other junior colleges struggle to provide regular advising for students. At Arrupe, advising happens during the summer enrichment program, formally several times a semester, and informally each day. Sean again: "The faculty role is unusual here by virtue of the depth of our involvement with student advising. We are classroom instructors, but our advising role brings *cura personalis* to the heart of our work. Our advising goes beyond formal meetings and a focus on logistics like registration, financial aid, and navigating student services. We faculty members relate with students differently, in accordance with our various personalities and styles, but we all are open to students with whatever challenges, questions, anxieties, or enthusiasms they bring to us. Sometimes this means helping students write an email to a professor or administrator. Other times this means encouraging them not to get discouraged by a bad grade. Still other times it means just chatting about music. Arrupe's advising model works because the students can tell everyone here cares about them and wants to know what's going on."

Philosophy instructor Minerva Ahumada further reflects on faculty availability, which she calls "intersections": "I have office hours most days of the week. But from 1:00 to 2:00 p.m., office hours or not, my office receives an influx of students: morning students on their way out, afternoon students on their way in. Some of the students come in with questions: there's an administrative task they need help with, the reflection that is due that night is not totally clear, there's a situation at home they'd like to discuss. But most of the students just come in to say hi, to talk about how their day is going, and to see if I have cookies. (I keep cookies on a shelf by the door.) I like the intensity of this hour because of the countless trajectories that conversations take in sixty minutes; it reminds me of cooking lessons with my mom; this is what she meant by a rolling boil. Office hours are probably my favorite thing at Arrupe, as it has been there that I have learned to listen to my students and have felt challenged to be a better teacher in class and adviser outside the classroom."

Minerva, like most of us at Arrupe, has worked with students who have been under-represented in higher education. In Minerva's case, she taught at LaGuardia Community College in New York. "Arrupe and community colleges all over the United States are places that are trying to find a way to correct the social inequality that has made it harder for certain people to attend—or feel that they belong at—a four-college or university," she says. "Students who come to Arrupe represent a segment of the population that desires to be educated but who also need education that suits their needs—financially, emotionally, and intellectually. Because Arrupe is such a small place, these ideas are not just political platforms but realities."

Minerva's colleagues reflected on various highlights during their first year at Arrupe. Math instructor Kate Nissan states, "The absolute highlight for me is without a doubt, the amazing and awe inspiring students." English instructor Daniel Burke agrees. "Nearly all of the best moments of the past year have taken place in the classroom, when an activity or reading has sparked an engaged and revelatory discussion with my students. Most often it happens when students find a way to overlay something we're reading in a text onto their daily lives outside the classroom."

Julia Bninski teaches English and writing. She initiated an African American Read-In at Arrupe.

This event was founded in 1990 by the Black Caucus of the National Council of Teachers of English. Its goal is to celebrate African American literature and to incorporate literature and literacy into Black History Month. With support from the Loyola library system, we hosted our first Read-In during February 2016. About thirty students attended, and probably half of them read aloud from African American books that they had brought or borrowed. I don't think I've ever seen such an attentive audience. These young people were truly engaged as they listened to their peers share literature that was important to them. It was enough to make any teacher jealous.

Associate dean Jennie Boyle's highlights influenced the trajectory of our college. Arrupe's original instructional design consisted of students enrolling for only two classes, eight weeks at a time. Classes ran for three hours per meeting. "We identified the eight-week sessions as problematic for the attainment of student learning objectives," recalls Jennie. "While we had more time on paper, in reality our three-hour class meetings amounted to two and a half hours of productive work in the classroom; eight weeks (including finals) was not enough time to utilize Ignatian pedagogical principles to meet course learning objectives." Jennie, the faculty, and I realized early on that the model didn't work, that our students needed more time to absorb the material presented in class. I appreciate the nimbleness of my colleagues in making the change. "We decided to move to a traditional semester with fifteen weeks of instruction in order to help students move beyond memorization to critically evaluate, reflect, and respond to knowledge. This affords students more time to prepare for entrance to a four-year university where they will need to manage more than two courses in a given term."

As we anticipated an incoming freshmen class—over one thousand students applied for 180 seats—Jennie and the faculty began the process of hiring new faculty. "Seven of us hired nine new faculty," she reports. "Because of our shared values and shared sense of mission, we were able to recruit talented teacher-scholars who shared our values and commitment to mission." Of our fifteen faculty members at Arrupe, seven are people of color.

Among the shared values and mission Jennie describes, one is my Martha vs. Mary vision from Luke's Gospel—not doing for, but being with. Minerva Ahumada articulates her experience of this during her office hours at Arrupe: "Understanding students at Arrupe in this way has led me to see myself as a companion on their journey. Not a guide, but a companion. Because of this, I know that I am not the wisest person in my office, that I am changed by their presence and gifts, and while I hope to use my knowledge in service of their educational and personal goals, they use their experiences in making me a more careful and observant person."

Hiring a College Placement Director

> *Life is not easy for any of us. But what of that? We must have perseverance and, above all, confidence in ourselves. We must believe that we are gifted for something and that this something must be attained.*
>
> —Marie Curie

February of our first year was an important marker. Loyola University approved my request for a college placement director. While this position was not originally anticipated, I have come to believe that it is absolutely critical for our students, who, like their counterparts at Loyola and around the country, require guidance in applying to a four-year college once they complete their associate's degree with us. Some, we imagine, will continue at Loyola University. Others may want or need to transfer to another four-year program. All will need a strong advocate to help them find the right fit and resources.

Getting this position approved was an uphill battle. Not because people didn't care. The problem is summarized by the questions asked by a well-meaning administrator at Loyola: "Why a college placement director? Why does Arrupe need this? Don't the students already have faculty members as advisers?" But if students from other backgrounds needed assistance navigating a transfer, why should Arrupe students settle for assistance from faculty advisers, who are heroic but unqualified as college counselors. Some of this stems from the outdated "mom and pop" model, in which well-meaning, hardworking personnel take on responsibilities for which they have little to no training. The result—burned out colleagues and mixed outcomes. The stakes are too high in post-secondary education—and for Arrupe students.

In building the job description for the college placement director, I required applicants to have at least three years of experience in the field. A human resources person at Loyola pointed out that I'd listed Spanish language ability as desirable but not required, and wondered if that should be at the top of the list. Knowing Spanish would certainly be a plus, I countered, but what's critical is that we hire a professional who can assist our students get into four-year colleges and universities—and find the right financial packages and support services that will ensure retention and graduation. Informing my sense of urgency was Scott Carlson's article, "Poor Kids, Limited Horizons: The Support They Need to Overcome Barriers to Aspirational Careers Comes Too Little, Too Late," in the January 22 issue of the

Chronicle of Higher Education. Carlson cites a college placement director, Katherine Pastor, who says, "Teachers, counselors, or family members can sometimes counsel a student past the limits they see for themselves, but often not." Often our students don't see themselves at competitive colleges and universities and private, selective institutions like Loyola because they don't know anyone attending them. When they hear the price tag—thirty thousand dollars, forty thousand dollars, or more—they are overwhelmed. Their sticker shock prevents them from pursuing scholarships and robust financial-aid packages. The good news is that during the first year of Arrupe's existence, as they grow in confidence, experience success, and find their coursework stimulating and relevant, our students see themselves as college students. Almost all of them express a desire to go on to a four-year program after they earn their associate's degree from Arrupe College. This is going to be tricky in a lot of cases, because they will be accustomed to paying under two thousand dollars a year for college. Hence, the need for a professional to guide them.

Then there's the issue of what kind of support four-year universities can offer our students once they are accepted. Let me give an example. The president of a small, elite, liberal arts college in the Midwest visited Arrupe in December 2015 and spoke with Maggie and me. He was very personable and very sincere in his desire to accept Arrupe students. He said that he recognized that his small liberal arts college missed out on a lot of great young people, the kind of students who are enrolled in Arrupe. I was very impressed with his sincerity and the success he's experienced leading an outstanding college with a terrific brand. But when I asked what kinds of services the school could offer students like ours, who are good students but need extra support, he responded, "We have an enviable student-to-teacher ratio." "Our faculty members are really committed to the students." I shook my head. That's not enough. I wanted to hear more. I asked him how many of our students he would be willing to accept. Then I explained that he should consider taking five of our students at a time because being a transfer student, no matter who they are or where they're from, is challenging, especially when they transfer as juniors.

I discussed this later with a friend who said, "You know, Steve, you want to hire a college placement director who will press colleges and college presidents, who will make a strong case for why your well-prepared students of color should go to their college or university, who will ensure that the four-year schools have the right kind of support and services to help your graduates complete their degrees and move on to successful careers. In short, you want to hire a badass."

Maggie and Derek led the search and brought in several strong candidates for me to review. I hired Julie Garcia, who previously served as the college counselor at a Catholic high school for girls in Chicago. Julie's experience in placing students from low-income backgrounds in four-year institutions impressed me—she knows how to find money for students who otherwise could never afford to go on to college. Julie loves the mission of Arrupe College, and she has the professional experience and training our students deserve.

As soon as Julie began, she was off and running—literally, as she was training for the Chicago marathon—because I tasked her with creating a college tour for Arrupe students. When I worked at Loyola School in Manhattan, our college counselor, Tom Hanley, led week-long college tours for our students—one week visiting New England colleges and universities, another week touring Mid-Atlantic institutions. Loyola School students returned as better-informed consumers. "I want to stay urban," they would opine; or "I'd like a smaller school"; or "I want to stick with the Jesuits"; or "I'm ready for a big research school experience."

I wanted the same experience for Arrupe students.

Julie spoke with Tom and began to design trips to schools in Missouri, Indiana, and Wisconsin. The first trip was an overnight to Saint Louis, the next was another overnight to South Bend, and the third was two days in Wisconsin. "SLU was great, Father," Cristobal said upon his return from the Missouri road trip. "I felt comfortable there because it's Jesuit, like we are." Edie was over the moon about Saint Mary's, across the street from Notre Dame. "I loved it there, Father, and I think its nursing program could be great for me." Victoria came back from Wisconsin glowing about Ripon. "It's small and intimate," she said, and then, after a pause, she looked at me and said, "I could see myself there." The key ingredient: belonging. Whether Arrupe grads continue their studies at Loyola University or transfer to another four-year college, they will want the feeling of belonging that we inculcate here.

PART 4

The Students

Building a Culture
of Accompaniment and Belonging

Building a Culture of Belonging

We don't prevent you from experiencing those bad things; instead, we try to change the meaning of them, so that they don't mean to you that things are never going to get better.
—DAVID YEAGER

By February 2016 I realized that one of my top challenges was building a culture. We enjoy a close relationship with Loyola University, because we are a college within the university, even though we are unique because we are serving a different population. The Loyola culture is not congruent with the Arrupe culture. The average high school grade point average of our first class was 2.7; the average ACT score was 17. Arrupe students' classmates enrolled in Loyola's college of arts and sciences held average GPAs of 3.7 and average ACTs of 27. What, then, would be the culture of a college whose students couldn't afford ACT prep classes in high school? What would be the culture for students coming from some high schools that were under resourced and underperforming? How do Arrupe students belong in the larger Loyola University Chicago culture?

I wanted our culture to be based not on failure or frustration but on achievement. Not about biases or stereotypes or pity, but rather about Arrupe students being co-creators as we build a new college community and a new culture. But first, our students needed to own their identities as young women and men enrolled in a selective, competitive, Jesuit liberal arts environment. They needed to feel as though they belonged.

Easier said than done for first-generation students of color commuting to classes at a majority white school where their counterparts live on campus and are the daughters and sons of parents who graduated from college. Author Paul Tough describes this tension in "Who Gets to Graduate from College?" which appeared in the *New York Times* magazine in May 2014. The article highlights the work of University of Texas researcher David Yeager. David works with young people who fit the Arrupe profile. The students arrive at college wondering if they will fit in, if they belong there. If the initial round of grades from tests or written assignments are low, they feel their self-doubts have been confirmed. When students fail a test or struggle in a class, they perceive their failures or struggles as permanent, personal, and pervasive. Things won't improve. The failure confirms that they don't belong in higher education. These negative experiences, in their estimation, will only continue; in fact, they will cascade. For some students, seeking tutoring and support is a shameful experience and further confirmation that they don't belong. Parents without the benefit of their own college careers can't draw from their experience and say, "My first semester was a huge adjustment. Who's your adviser? Is it too late to drop this class? When does your instructor have office hours?" Instead, they see their son or daughter suffering, or they hear their frustration during phone conversations, and they counsel their child to come home.

David and his colleagues at UT Austin offer an alternative. They attempt to change the student's mindset. Instead of interpreting a failed test as permanent, personal, and pervasive, the student is encouraged to think of the event as a situation that is specific and transient. Yes, failing your first test as an undergrad is lousy, but it's one specific test. The student is asked to consider any obstacles that prevented him or her from being successful. Once obstacles are identified, the student is asked what can be done so that the outcome will be different for the next test. After reading the article, I reached out to David. "Do you ever get to Chicago?" I asked. "My wife is from Chicago," David replied, "and my in-laws like it when I visit." I paused. "I'll tell you what, David. If you help me, I'll help your marriage."

When we eventually met, I described the students I was anticipating working with at Arrupe College. David responded by explaining that in his experience, students like ours are motivated to attend college not because their salaries will be better or because their lifetime earnings will be higher. Rather, they believe with their degree they can be of greater service to their younger siblings, to their grandparents, to their neighborhoods, to the kids at their old high school. They're very altruistic. I responded that this attitude is consistent with our school's patron, Fr. Pedro Arrupe and his goal to form students to become men and women for and with others. David's face fell, and he said, "I've gotta tell you, I went to Notre Dame, and I was taught by the Basilian Fathers down in Texas, so I'm not good with all this Jesuit stuff." I replied, "If you're going to be on the payroll, you'd better get good with it, because you're going to be talking this Jesuit stuff at Arrupe College." We laughed. And David became a major influencer of our culture.

We designed a survey that was administered to Arrupe students in December of our first year to determine if they felt they belonged at our college. The first statement read: "I feel confident that I belong at Arrupe." The possible answers ranged from not at all true to completely true. Forty-five percent of our students checked completely true, while 34 percent indicated very true. Another question, "Sometimes I wonder if I don't belong at Arrupe College," received a 53.5 percent response of not at all true. Encouraging responses.

The survey provided us with other data. Students often see their first low grade as permanent rather than as just one point in time. Our survey addressed this. "You only have a certain amount of intelligence, and you really cannot do much to change it," we stated. Thirty percent strongly disagreed; 28 percent disagreed; 18.5 percent mostly disagreed; 7 percent agreed; and 2 percent strongly agreed. Hmmm. Another statement from the survey: "You can learn new things, but you really cannot change whether you are smart or not." Thirty-one percent strongly disagreed; 24.5 percent disagreed; 18.5 percent mostly disagreed; almost 10 percent agreed; and 4 percent strongly agreed. Yet another: "You can grow your basic intelligence over the course of your lifetime." Forty percent strongly agreed; 35 percent agreed; and 17.5 percent mostly agreed.

To counter misconceptions that struggling demonstrates an innate lack of ability, David coached our faculty at Arrupe to use statements that emphasize that intelligence is a lifelong activity. When a student struggles, David suggests adding *yet* to a negative self-assessment, for example, "I just don't get it *yet.*" We don't have to be better than other classmates in a particular discipline, just better than where we started from. The point is we may not "get it" right away, but we can grow our understanding step by step. David rehearsed lines like this with Arrupe faculty during his first visit to our college: "So you got a low score. It is just a measure of what you can do right now, not a measure of what you can ever do." Finally, David suggests phrasing critical feedback carefully. He cautioned us to avoid saying, "Well, you may not be good in this subject." Instead, he recommended this alternative: "This class has a high standard of really deeply understanding the material. But I would not hold you to it if I did not believe that together we could get there."

A few weeks after David worked with our faculty, I asked Luisa, a 4.0 student, how she was doing in her courses. She sighed and then admitted, "Well, Father, I've got an 88 in oral communication." I said, "Luisa, that's a good grade. You seem dissatisfied or concerned." She replied, "Father, I have a high standard." David Yeager was influencing our students, our interactions with them, and our culture.

Family Night

May hope fill your heart and shine a light on all the possibilities God has in store for you.
—GRANDMOTHER OF AN ARRUPE STUDENT

Parents' Weekend is a feature of many colleges and universities. Scheduled about a month or six weeks after classes begin, Parents' Weekend offers abundant activities and opportunities for mothers and fathers to get a feel for their child's classes, roommate(s), and college life. Parents socialize with other parents and perhaps with campus administrators. A ritual seems to be going shopping for items needed for the dorm room, followed by a celebratory meal at an off-campus restaurant with students, roommates, and family members breaking bread, building community, building networks, and deepening affinity for the college or university.

As posters advertising Loyola University's Parents' Weekend were displayed across the university's buildings, including Maguire Hall, which houses Arrupe, I was concerned that there would be no Parents' Weekend for Arrupe College students. For starters, our students don't live in residence halls—they're commuters. There would be no big restaurant dinners or visits with roommates or trips to Bed, Bath, and Beyond. Yolanda Golden and I agreed that we should do something—we should have an alternative for Parents' Weekend. Yolanda came up with Family Night—a catered event to which students could bring their parents, their grandparents, and any family members they wanted.

Nicolas brought his sister Mercedes, who was eleven, and his other sister Angelica, who was five or six. It was certainly Family Night for them, and I was pleased Nicolas felt comfortable bringing them to our event. Grandmothers, mothers, aunts, boyfriends, all were welcomed. Along with opportunities to eat and to socialize with faculty and staff, one of our faculty members, Daniel Burke, ran Bingo with John Buethe, our academic services coordinator. It's come to this, I thought—Bingo. "Boy," I said aloud. "Tonight, we have our Catholic identity—we're having Bingo." The students and their family members loved it. We also featured another hallmark of Catholic organizations: raffles. A nice evening—and a meaningful alternative, Arrupe style, to Parents' Weekend.

Sometimes I think I'm overly sensitive about our students' perceptions, whether they feel they belong or not. Maybe I'm overthinking all this. A few months after our Family Night, however, I was given food for thought. A colleague runs a support group for young men enrolled at Arrupe called the Brotherhood. My colleague reported that a few members of the Brotherhood, in referring to Loyola University's main campus where the majority of undergrads live in residence halls, said, "That's not for us, right?" My colleague probed, and the Arrupe students saw themselves as being different from other Loyola University undergrads. It's a different experience at Arrupe. Our students face challenges and balance competing claims that they perceive as being different from the daily reality of a typical Jesuit university student. I am learning a lot about Jesuit higher education from the Arrupe student community—on Family Night and every other night and day.

Laptops

I am really happy and thankful for the laptops that you have given to us. You are contributing to making my dream of going to college become a reality. I am the first one in my family to attend college. I am enjoying Arrupe College because it is helping me and encouraging me to work hard so I can graduate. The faculty have been helping me on my assignments so I can succeed in my classes. I am really proud that I was accepted here. I am happy that there are people like you willing to help students like me.

—Arrupe student

Classes began at Arrupe College on August 17, 2015. Three days later, on August 20, we distributed laptops to all of our students. Our associate dean for academics, Jennie Boyle, had decided on laptops instead of tablets because laptops offer more versatility. In addition, whether our students had tablets, desktops, laptops, or nothing, the gift of the same model of laptops meant everyone would be at the same starting point for technology. Faculty were also issued laptops for instructional purposes.

Pam and George Hamel, my friends in California, made a very generous gift to Arrupe College in January 2015, and part of their gift covered the cost of these laptops. When we met with the students to give them out, I had just seen the movie *Mission Impossible* with Tom Cruise. I recommended the film to the students. "I'd hate to be Tom Cruise in this movie," I continued, "because his character can't trust anyone. He can't trust his love interest because she might be a double agent. He can't trust his allies because they might be ready to turn him in. He can't trust anyone." I then said to the students: "We want to trust you. My friends Pam and George in California have decided to give you laptops. But they asked me, 'Can we trust your students to take care of the laptops?' and I responded, 'This will be the big test!'"

I asked the students, "What happens if you lose the laptop, or if it breaks, or if you loan it to someone, or if it disappears somehow?" They said without missing a beat, "Well, Father, we'll lose your trust." "That's right," I said. "People said it was 'mission impossible' to start Arrupe College. It would be more of a 'mission impossible' for us to run Arrupe College if we could not trust you, so we look forward to seeing what you do with these computers. Here are your laptops."

The students were stunned. As we distributed the laptops, one student, Randall, looked at me incredulously and asked, "Are these really for us?" Another student, who was homeless at the time (since then we have helped get her situated at Mercy Home for Boys and Girls), rallied some of her classmates to write thank-you notes for the laptops. This gave me pause—and hope. Someone who is homeless and should be overwhelmed with all that she doesn't have in life was interested in saying thank you for what she was given. What an extraordinary woman!

That same night one of the students, Khaled, wrote the following email to me: "Fr. Katsouros, this is Khaled. I want to thank you on behalf of Arrupe students for having faith in us. I promise we will try to maintain and grow this trust as we progress. We thank you and your friends for providing the laptops; it means a lot to us. Thank you. Khaled." I shared the email with my colleagues and with Pam and George. *Mission impossible?* More like *mission important.*

Making the Grade:
You Have to Fight for This

If you're walking down the right path, and you're willing to keep walking, eventually you'll make progress.
—Barack Obama

On October 28, 2015, after the end of the first session of classes at Arrupe College, we held a town hall meeting for all our students. I shared with them that 82 percent of them had completed two classes by the end of the first session. I complimented those students, telling them that they were already ahead of the other undergraduates, the other freshmen, their classmates at Loyola University who were taking classes in the regular traditional semester schedule. I then announced that 48 percent of our students had achieved a GPA of 2.85 or higher. A 2.85 GPA is one of our benchmark goals for our students at Arrupe College. I also told them that thirty-nine of our students had made the dean's list.

What was wonderful to see was that students who weren't on the dean's list, who had not achieved a 2.85, who had not completed two classes in the first session, were applauding for their classmates who had. The previous weekend I'd heard a talk delivered by Benedictine Sister Joan Chittister. She had started her remarks with a joke I enjoyed, and I shared it with the students, admitting that it was kind of cheesy but asking them to stick with me, because it fits our situation at Arrupe:

A priest and a rabbi are going to a boxing match together at Madison Square Garden in New York. One of the boxers is Jewish, and the other one is Catholic. The Jewish boxer comes into the ring, beats his fist on his chest, flexes his muscles, and goes to his corner of the ring. The Catholic boxer comes to the center of the ring, beats his chest, flexes his muscles, and goes to his corner of the ring. Before he does, however, he makes the sign of the cross. The rabbi, watching all of this, turns to the priest and, copying the Catholic boxer's sign of the cross, asks, "Does this help?" The priest responds, "Only if he can fight."

I said to our students, "I can pray for you, and we can support you, and we can provide you with great faculty who are very generous with their time and their talent. We can provide you with a jobs counselor, with coaches, with a social worker, with computers, with a meal program, but you have to fight for this. Only if you are willing to fight are you going to be able to pull this off."

I reminded the students that nationally only 5 percent of those enrolled in two-year colleges graduate in two years; that in Chicago only 17 percent of those enrolled in two-year colleges graduate in two years. I told the students, "I don't want you to be in the 83 percent that doesn't complete. But you have to fight for it."

A number of the students had seen the movie *The Martian*. I reminded them how Matt Damon's character gets left behind for dead on Mars but fights against all odds until his crew mates return to rescue him. "We'll come back for you, we'll walk with you, we'll accompany you," I said to the Arrupe students, "but like Matt Damon's character, you've got to show some fight, show some life."

Three months later, on January 27, 2016, we held our academic convocation at Arrupe College. We acknowledged the students who were on the dean's list. Earlier in the year, as an incentive, I had announced that each member of the dean's list would be assigned one of the roomy, old school wooden lockers on the first floor of our building, Maguire Hall, vestiges of the building's days as Loyola's law school. I then gave these students the combinations to their new lockers. It was a rewarding moment to see their excitement and pride in their accomplishment. Who knew wooden lockers would be a meaningful incentive? It worked.

But along with the rewards of seeing our students succeed, I'm constantly concerned about how to encourage those students who are struggling academically. In the weeks leading up to the academic convocation, I racked my brain and rallied any troops I could find to help me think of ways to honor students who were struggling but fighting the good fight. What would incentivize their progress? We wanted to honor students who had earned their way off academic probation, so we developed the forward achievement award. This award is for students who have fought their way back, who have, as the African American folk saying goes, "made a way out of no way." *Forward* originates from President Obama's reelection campaign in 2012. I thought that would be appropriate, given that he's a son of Chicago and we want all of our students to move forward. So these students received forward achievement award certificates.

But what about those students who were still struggling with finding a way forward? What would be their "wooden lockers"? How would they achieve them? Earlier in the month I was talking about all of this with my friend Dan Cardinali. Dan connected me with a colleague, Heather Clawson, who is the vice president of research, evaluation, and innovation at Communities in Schools. Heather and I discussed how we can motivate and not discourage those students who have yet to be successful. We kicked around some ideas, some shorter-term growth metrics that we could use to encourage our students.

John Buethe, our academic coordinator, identified other benchmarks that we were able to announce at the convocation, such as honoring students for "midterm eight-week growth." Later that spring, we acknowledged students who achieved growth of greater than 0.60. We also honored students who use Arrupe's academic and social supports, such as seeing a tutor more than three hours a week; going to the writing center more than three hours a week; working with Farrah Ellison-Moore, our career coordinator, or our social worker, Jessica Wein, for more than three hours a week. Finally, the key ingredient: attendance—honoring students who improved their attendance by being present more than 85 percent of the time.

As for incentives, we kicked around all kinds of things from special meals to fun outings to field trips. We're looking to motivate our students, especially those we're at the greatest risk of losing. By January 2016, the time of the academic convocation, we were down to 149 students from our original 159. People were saying, "not bad." But our goal was to retain 85 percent of the students; that meant that by August 2016, the start of sophomore year, we needed to re-enroll 135 of the original 159 freshmen.

Thanks to Lidia Bastianich's generosity, on March 29, 2016, we hosted our second of two evenings at Lidia's wonderful Eataly restaurant with students whose GPA and attendance records improved earlier in the winter. Twelve students attended. One student, Ernesto, arrived wearing a great-looking bow tie. He had taken seriously my request to look sharp for the dinner. And then I looked at his shoes. I've never seen shoes polished as well as his. We complimented his sense of style; I could tell this dinner was very meaningful for Ernesto.

During the meal we shared plates. Audrey fell in love with mozzarella; Marcus devoured the agnoletti pasta with pork. Other students liked the ravioli. Then the desserts arrived; one was tiramisu. Dashaun, who had been homeless and was living at Mercy Home, took one bite of the tiramisu, looked lovingly at the remainder, and asked, "Tiramisu, where have you been all my life?" Hilarious. I responded, "Waiting for you, Dashaun."

Eataly is a few blocks from Arrupe College, so we walked to and from the restaurant that lovely evening. As we were saying our goodnights, Ernesto lingered to say, "Father, what a great evening, thanks so much." I loved his presence of mind, his shiny, well-polished shoes, his beautiful red bow tie, and his warm farewell. The end of a perfect evening celebrating outstanding young women and men.

Networks and Support Programs

If you are not proximate, you cannot change the world.
—Bryan Stevenson

In *Our Kids*, author Robert Putnam notes that the differences between those young people whose parents went to college and those whose parents didn't are striking. Primary among these differences is that young people whose parents attended college benefit from networks. Parents can contact friends about internships for their children, or they can reach out to a colleague who went to a particular college to put in a good word for their child. Our students often don't have those kinds of networks. I remind the board and the leaders of Arrupe College that we are the networks for the Arrupe students.

When I worked at Nativity, the Graduate Support Program was probably my first experience with *cura personalis*, a notion discussed several times in this book, meaning care for the whole person or a holistic view of the student's education. We attempted to provide for the young men of Nativity even after they graduated, to accompany them in their high school years and beyond. That accompaniment also included tuition support. At Arrupe, we are providing wrap-around services. In addition to faculty, Arrupe students benefit from the services offered by a career coordinator who works with the students on their job skills, on their presentation skills, on building a resume, on their interviewing skills, and on landing and keeping a job or an internship. In addition, we have a social worker, and we have access to Loyola's School of Social Work. When I first interviewed for the dean's position, Mike Garanzini and I talked about how Arrupe would share a building with another college or department at Loyola, and he suggested the School of Education. I knew that Loyola had a School of Social Work. I suggested that it might be a more pertinent neighbor. Mike agreed. The School of Social Work moved into Maguire Hall, where Arrupe is located, in 2016, and we look forward to great synergy between the master's of social work (MSW) students at Loyola, who need hours, and our students, who can benefit from MSW services. Our first social worker, Jessica Wein, served as a bridge between the School of Social Work and Arrupe College. Her successor, Ernest Fernandez, began after Jessica relocated to New York.

We also provide tutoring services, and we have a student disabilities officer. Arrupe is primarily an academic, credit-bearing degree program, and we want to provide the support pro- grams that will care for our students, their whole person, and ensure their success—*cura personalis.*

Jesuits are also an important part of the Arrupe College network. I find it very gratifying and very moving that the Society of Jesus is so invested in Arrupe College. Yes, with money, yes, with a building, and yes, with Loyola's resources, but also with personnel. There are so few Jesuits now and so many needs, so many requests for Jesuits. Yet when I ask my Jesuit brothers at Loyola to help interview students in the admissions process or to tutor students, my requests are always met with great generosity.

As I mentioned in my overview of the DLG meetings, Loyola University has a large Jesuit community that includes young

Jesuit scholastics in first studies, usually a combination of philosophy and theology. Three of these Jesuits began volunteering for us in September 2015, and I'm excited to report that one of them, Eric Immel, is continuing to work with us for the next two to three years as his regency assignment before he goes on to theology studies in preparation for ordination to the priesthood. After many conversations with Fr. Tim Lannon, SJ, the provincial assistant for formation for the Midwest Jesuits, Tim recommended to the provincials, Fr. Brian Paulson (Chicago-Detroit Province) and Fr. Tom Lawler (Wisconsin Province), that Eric be assigned to Arrupe College for his regency. Eric knows Loyola University and has a background in student services. He is very charismatic, smart, and intrusive in the best sense; he's not afraid to call a student to be accountable. Eric now serves as assistant dean, working closely with Yolanda Golden, our associate dean for student success.

Our tutors represent another vital part of our network and support system. I've been blessed with some great friendships since arriving in Chicago, and high on the list is the Borah family. Clare and Tom Borah are parishioners at Saints Faith, Hope, and Charity, where I celebrate mass on weekends. They are wonderfully supportive. Clare's parents, Rosemary and John Croghan, are terrific leaders in Chicago and have been instrumental in the founding and flourishing of Cristo Rey Jesuit High School and the Cristo Rey Network. Tom has been tutoring an Arrupe student named Dennis, who struggles academically. Tom is very dedicated, even using his lunch hour to work with Dennis. I've mentioned that my friend Jay tutored a student named Vincent. A colleague of mine, Rochelle, from the School of Communications, mentors a young woman named Raina. And the roster of tutors is growing. Wherever I go, people ask how they can help students at Arrupe College. My response: "The best thing you can do is to tutor a student for an hour a week or more if you can."

One of our undocumented students, Cristobal, is a strong-willed, talented young man. He's also a great advocate for himself and others. As a networker, he became involved with Chicago Scholars, another advocacy group that helps students get into colleges after high school. Derek Brinkley, our associate director for admissions, recently received a note from the director of College Persistence at Chicago Scholars, complimenting Cristobal:

> I just had a conversation with one of our students, Cristobal. He's a first-year student at Arrupe. He spoke so highly of his experience at Arrupe, particularly of his experience as an undocumented student at Arrupe. He feels supported, connected to the community, and the Lake Shore campus, and has received superb guidance and support from the financial aid office. I am so appreciative of institutions like Arrupe and Loyola University Chicago who are advocates for our students on a holistic level and truly do their part to impact their persistence day in and day out. Thank you for the work that you do to contributes to scholars like this having had such a meaningful experience. Chicago Scholars appreciates it. Please extend this thanks to your colleagues who I don't know. I really want them to know that they are appreciated as well.

One network that we have exercised since opening last summer is with Fr. Scott Donahue, the executive director of the Mercy Home for Boys and Girls. Mercy Home provides many crucial services for young people between the ages of eleven and twenty-one, including residences for homeless youth. One of our students, Lourdes, was living at Mercy Home before she enrolled at Arrupe. Another student, Edie, was living in an unsustainable situation with an elderly relative. When we learned of her situation, I visited Mercy Home. Scott rolled out the red carpet, introducing me to his team and hosting me during a tour of the facilities. I immediately saw a partnership with Mercy Home as a mutually beneficial relationship. Mercy Home provides a stable living environment, and we provide an educational opportunity for the older members of their residence. Edie now lives at Mercy Home and loves it. I am very impressed with this young woman and the many students who exhibit and exude extraordinary resilience.

I have more stories about Mercy Home and the challenges our students face. I share two of them in the following section.

Hurdles, Homelessness, and Self-Sabotage

You were taught to put away your former way of life, your old self.

—Ephesians 4:22

In the fall of 2015, after we had just completed our first session of classes, I hosted a happy hour celebration at the local McCormick and Schmick's restaurant for our faculty and staff. After the get together, I returned to Arrupe to pick up something from my office and ran into one of our students, Donnel. Donnel looked very disheveled and distracted, so I asked, "What's up?" He explained that his mother had thrown him out of the house. "Why?" I asked. Donnel explained that his mother is a drug addict. Donnel has a work-study job at Loyola University. This particular day was payday, and his mother demanded his paycheck to pay for her fix. I got the impression this wasn't the first time Donnel's mother had made this request. Today, however, Donnel finally refused and consequently his mother kicked him out of the house. Mercy Home is not just a nice entry in our rolodex of networks—for Donnel, Mercy Home provided a port in the storm of his personal life, except . . .

Donnel ended up saying no to the Mercy Home opportunity. While I thought it was the best option for him, what matters is what he thought. Donnel is the oldest of three siblings. His younger sister is a junior in high school, and their little brother attends elementary school. "I appreciate what you're trying to do for me, and Mercy Home is really nice, but I can't leave them, Fr. K," Donnel explained. Hmm. I cannot imagine the moral calculus Donnel faced. I am humbled by his selflessness.

Donnel's classmate, Dashaun, provides the second Mercy Home story. Dashaun is a very personable skateboarder and artist who struggles academically. And for good reason—he has a very unstable and abusive home environment. When we learned that Dashaun had left home and was sleeping in the lobbies of residence halls at Loyola University, Yolanda Golden and I sprang into action.

I contacted Scott Donahue at Mercy Home. Dashaun was already scheduled for an interview later in the month. I asked if there was any way Dashaun could interview sooner. This was a Friday evening, and I heard back immediately from one of Mercy Home's social workers that they would move the interview to the following Monday. The power of networks. In the meantime Yolanda had contacted Loyola University's residence-life department and was able to secure a temporary room for Dashaun at Loyola's Lake Shore campus. Arrupe's financial model does not include housing, an additional twelve thousand dollars. For an emergency—and Dashaun was an emergency—Dashaun was able to live temporarily in a residence hall at Loyola University's Lake Shore campus.

Once he got settled, Dashaun loved his room in the Loyola University residence hall. An empty triple, it was the largest room he'd ever occupied. When Dashaun connected with Minerva Ahumada, our philosophy professor with whom

Dashaun is close, he raved about the size of his room. However, on Monday morning Dashaun had an appointment at Mercy Home for his interviews. He overslept.

Farrah Ellison-Moore, our career counselor, and I spoke about how frustrating this situation was. We discussed how Dashaun was making progress at Arrupe and in his life, but he wasn't accustomed to making this kind of progress. Sleeping in and missing appointments can be a form of self-sabotage. Dashaun was getting close to a turning point in his life, and he wasn't entirely prepared for it. Mercy Home is accustomed to working with young people like Dashaun, so Scott contacted me when Dashaun completed the interview process and was moving into Mercy Home.

At the time I was writing this story, my mind was on the gospel for the first Sunday in Lent: the temptation of Jesus. Dashaun helped me understand the gospel in a new way. He was being invited to a new life, a different kind of life, and, we hoped, a better life. God invites us to be the people that God wants us to be. And yet the temptation is to stay stuck, to self-sabotage, to not accept God's invitation.

At least for now, Dashaun lives at Mercy Home. He did not default to self-sabotage. We have fingers crossed and candles lit that his residency at Mercy Home and his experience at Arrupe College will help him withstand whatever temptations prevent him from being the good young man he is, the good young man God invites him to be.

Stick with It

Grit is a passionate commitment to a single mission and an unswerving dedication to serve that mission.
　　　　　　　—PAUL TOUGH, *How Children Succeed*

In early February 2016 we enjoyed a visit from the White Foundation. I had met with Steve White from the foundation previously through Dixie Ost, a corporate and foundation relations officer at Loyola University's advancement office and a great supporter of Arrupe. From the start Steve has been very enthusiastic about Arrupe's mission, and his family's foundation provides scholarships for three of our students: Omar, Bernardo, and Ramon.

For Steve's visit Maggie Murphy Stockson and I asked the three students to meet with Steve and a guest of his, Euclid Williamson, who is the founder and executive director of Target H.O.P.E., a "nonprofit organization that creates innovative academic retention strategies to combat the high school dropout crisis and increase minority graduation rates in higher education." Right up our alley. It was a great conversation, one during which I became increasingly aware of our students' growth and also their influence on higher education. Their experiences and perceptions are informing Jesuit post-secondary education.

To prime the pump, I had asked the students questions before we opened it up for Steve and Euclid Williamson. One of my questions was, "While we are preparing to admit the class of 2018, next year's freshmen, what advice, what wisdom, would you share with them?" This is a great tactic for empowering our students. They are the experts now, and that gives them a sense that they've accomplished something in a short period of time.

Ramon, who is generally quieter than his classmates, said: "Stick it out. Stay focused on the future. That's my advice for the incoming freshmen." Ramon seemed to be channeling researcher Angela Duckworth, the author of *Grit*, who describes persistence and resilience as the key characteristics for success for students like ours, or for anyone.

For students from low-income backgrounds and high-crime neighborhoods, making the most of the opportunities that

Arrupe College offers requires the grit Duckworth describes. My money is on Ramon to, as he said to our guests, stick it out and stay focused.

Learning from Our Students

If you have come here to help me, you are wasting your time. But if you have come because your liberation is bound up with mine, then let us work together.
—LILLA WATSON, ABORIGINAL ELDER, ACTIVIST, ARTIST, AND EDUCATOR

One evening I enjoyed a dinner out with one of our adjuncts and his wife. The adjunct described how much he is learning from our students, articulating the language of Pope Francis, the language of accompaniment. I see all of us at Arrupe College accompanying one another as we launch the college, as we attempt to innovate higher education, as our students are taking courses, and as we are learning to be a college together.

One of our board members, Mark Shriver, is the uncle of Tim Shriver, Jr., who is the president of the Jesuit Volunteer Corps (JVC). Tim and I have become friends, and recently we were talking about JVC. He also has been very much influenced by Pope Francis and the language of accompaniment. One of his goals for the volunteers working in educational placements is to get away from the notion that education is transactional—that the teacher presents information and the student receives it.

As Tim was talking about his desires and dreams for JVC, it transported me back to when I was a graduate student at Loyola

University Chicago and studied the educational philosophy of American pragmatist John Dewey. Dewey's philosophy reminded me of Jesuit education as he wrote about meeting students where they are. The student is not an empty vessel that needs filling by the instructor; rather, the student brings his or her life experience and hopes and dreams to the classroom, and that's the starting point for the educational process.

That influenced my work in Harlem. I said to my students there, "Let's learn about Langston Hughes and James Walden Johnson, and Zora Neale Hurston and Walter F. White, Nella Larson and W. E. B. Du Bois and Claude McKay and Countee Cullen. They lived in the neighborhood where we live now." I'd ask my students, "Why was the Harlem Renaissance the Harlem Renaissance? And what do we need to do to recreate that Renaissance in Harlem now? Even better, what kind of renaissance do people in Harlem, people like us, need now?" The students and the location were the starting points for the curriculum. I still have a poster in my office from those days, depicting leaders of the Harlem Renaissance—a reminder of my desire to meet students where they are.

John Dewey influenced me during my years in Harlem. Pope Francis influences me in my work now. "The Church will have to initiate everyone . . . into this 'art of accompaniment' which teaches us to remove our sandals before the sacred ground of the other," the pope wrote in *Evangelii Gaudium*. Francis models a disposition that is present among my colleagues at Arrupe. We have learned so much about how to run our college from our students, from their needs and their backgrounds and their aspirations and their observations. They are contributing to the creation of Arrupe College. They are also contributing to Loyola University and to the landscape of Jesuit higher education. Pope Francis reminds me that I tread on sacred ground in Maguire Hall, made sacred by my colleagues and our students.

Praying and Kvelling

"But what about you?" Jesus asked. "Who do you say I am?"
—MARK 8:29

When I was back East during the holidays, I got together with friends who have invested in Catholic educations for their children. At one point during our visit, the patriarch of the family observed, "I have sent four of my five children to Catholic colleges and universities, and I'm very pleased with the outcomes. My children attended mass on their campuses and they participated in retreats and service trips. But my children didn't learn how to pray." He paused, and asked, "Why didn't my kids come out of Catholic schools knowing how to pray?"

A few days later I returned to Chicago and worked with fellow Jesuit Jamie Calder to plan a student retreat that we had in the works. We wanted to offer our students retreats at Loyola University Retreat and Ecology Campus (LUREC) in Woodstock, Illinois, which is where all of our students first started with orientation in the summer of 2015. I explained to Jamie that he'd take different advisory groups of twenty students each over the course of three consecutive Tuesdays and Wednesdays. Our three main goals were for our students to learn about St. Ignatius; about Pedro Arrupe; and about how to pray using tools such as the "Examen," the Ignatian daily prayer that emphasizes God's role in everyday activities.

After one of the retreats Maggie Murphy Stockson and I hosted a group of potential donors at Arrupe, and we invited two students to speak. One of the students, Ayesha, who is not Catholic, talked about the retreat and what a great experience it was for her. She said, "I was really grateful to be able to slow down and do some deep breathing, to become more mindful, to learn a little bit more about how to pray. I found that to be centered was something that I needed and something that I will continue now that the retreat is over. I want to integrate that into my lifestyle." When my friend with children who attended Catholic colleges heard this, he sighed and said, "I should have sent my kids to Arrupe!"

Jamie Calder's days of reflection were a great gift to be able to offer to students in any setting or environment—an opportunity to slow down. I've talked to the students about becoming contemplatives in action, and I have to admit we have the action down, but we haven't quite figured out the contemplative part. Jamie reached these students and, as Ayesha presented so well, they are learning how to pray.

One of my old routines from Loyola School in Manhattan was to join the students at the end of their retreats, share a meal, and do an exercise based on the gospel in which we ask, "Who do we say that we are?" Students would pull the name of a classmate out of a hat and then describe who they are and who the other person is. It's a simple affirmation exercise, and it requires students to represent themselves and to be thoughtful in their representation of someone else. We recreated this for the students at Arrupe College. One student whom I don't know very well, Sonya, really floored me with her response to the question, "Who do I say that I am?" She said, "I am the person who is dealing with all of the obstacles that I put in my life." Sonya is a mother who struggles to juggle school and child care. She feels burdened, but she finished by explaining how Arrupe College is an opportunity for her in spite of her "obstacles."

When drawing the name of a fellow student, Arianna drew the name of Philip, a student who can be socially awkward. Arianna spoke with great affection about Philip and said, "We know that when you are ready, you are going to be a high-impact player. You are really going to be this great presence among us." She was very encouraging. Then it was Philip's turn to talk about himself. He spoke haltingly about his behaviors. You could have heard a pin drop. The group of about thirty students, faculty, and staff were spellbound. Philip couldn't have participated in this exercise even a few weeks prior. The atmosphere of the retreat in particular and of Arrupe in general enabled Philip to speak as genuinely as he did.

Another student, Karen, described how she felt more academically confident. Karen was floundering academically at the end of our first session of eight-week classes in October 2015, but she turned it around and was acknowledged for her great academic progress with a forward achievement award certificate at the academic convocation a week and a half before the retreat. Karen shared that she was beginning to believe in herself and that she was interested in pursuing a career in medicine, maybe even in becoming a surgeon.

Keith also struggled academically earlier in the year. Still, he earned a forward achievement award certificate for academic progress during the second eight-week session from October to December 2015. It was very moving for me to witness these students growing before our very eyes. Keith, like Karen, was beginning to see himself as a college student. He noted during the retreat exercise that his experience at Arrupe provided him with new, positive perspectives about himself overall.

The last student to speak was Julio. Julio spoke very generously about his peers, saying how proud he was of them, how proud that he was their classmate, how they were all college material. But then he said something startling—that while he liked being at Arrupe, he did not consider himself worthy of being in college. I responded by telling him that he is an outstanding public speaker—something we value highly. Then I told him that what he said about himself and his classmates was extraordinary, and that he should not discount himself from being a college student. "You are contributing to our community," I told him. "Without you, we would be less than we are. We need you at

Arrupe, not just because of the nice things you say about your classmates, but because of who you are and because of the gift that you are to your classmates and to Arrupe College and to Loyola University."

During my Jesuit tertianship experience, I learned to pay attention to the full nets that Jesus promises Peter, James, and John in the gospel. Moments like those student reflections on retreat remind me that my nets are often bursting at Arrupe College. I'm reminded also of the Yiddish word *kvell*, which means "to be extraordinarily proud." During the student retreat I was kvelling for Sonya and Arianna, for Karen, Keith, Philip, and Julio, and for Arrupe College. My nets were full that day, and my heart is full as well when I think about our students.

PART 5

The Future

"See, I Make All Things New"

Wooing

It is easy to witness an awakening within the Arrupe student body as you see the students develop. They are no longer defined by their past or where they come from, but rather by their future and dreams, which are no longer impossibilities.
—ARRUPE COLLEGE BOARD MEMBER

There is no way to review our first year at Arrupe and not find some of what has happened to be incredible—truly beyond belief. For example, we had over one thousand students apply for entrance to the next year's class. Of the first four hundred we interviewed, we accepted 183. Given my love for statistics and numbers that tell a story, I am constantly reminded of the story told by our current numbers.

I am concerned that our numbers are skewed toward Latinos. I'm conscious of the fact that the population of Chicago is one-third African American, one-third Latino, and one-third Asian and white. We stressed during the last admissions season that we want to enroll more African Americans at Arrupe. In our second year Isabel Reyes and Derek Brinkley from our admissions office focused on visiting feeder schools with higher black enrollments; in some cases they recruited from schools that reported a 94–97 percent African American enrollment. They visited thirty-three high schools and revisited ten of those schools more than once. Their efforts seem to be paying off. Our inaugural class was composed of 70 percent Latino, 20 percent African American, 5 percent biracial, 3 percent white, and 2 percent Asian students.

The next class, however, is 60 percent Latino and 33 percent African American.

Some other numbers: We are 61 percent female and 39 percent male. We had 24 percent undocumented in the incoming 2016 class, which means we had forty-two kids in this group who did not qualify for Pell or for MAP Grants. That's on top of thirty-four undocumented students in our first freshman class. That translates into more fundraising!

Some of these students applied to the TheDream.US program, and others benefit from the support offered by the Pritzker Foundation, but I wonder how many of these students will need money for school and where that money will come from. We already have some generous donors. One board member of a foundation heard a homily about undocumented students I gave one Sunday, and that foundation came through with a $100,000 gift. We continue to pursue support for students who are ineligible for federal and state aid as a result of their citizenship status.

In our inaugural class, 45 percent of our students were graduates of Chicago public schools, 28 percent from Chicago Catholic schools, and 27 percent from Chicago charter schools. For the incoming 2016 class, 54 percent graduated from public schools, 25 percent from charter schools, and 21 percent from Catholic schools. I attribute this shift to our African American recruitment strategy. It also has been my experience that Catholic high schools brand themselves as college prep, and college for some students and their families does not mean two-year colleges. (Despite the best efforts of former President Obama and Mayor Emmanuel to extol the virtues of two-year colleges, they're still perceived as "less than.") We are also cognizant that the public is aware of the low retention and graduate rates of many two-year colleges. That definitely affects us negatively when trying to attract interest from some populations.

Financial aid is always an interesting set of numbers to parse. For the incoming class of 2016, we denied financial aid to ninety-four students, based on a number of reasons, the most common being that their expected family contribution was too high. We recruit students from low-income families.

Another reason for rejecting students for admission is a result of a poor interview during which they couldn't explain why they wanted to go to college, represent what interested them about Arrupe, or give examples demonstrating their perseverance or persistence or grit. And frankly, our interviewers assessed that some applicants would not be successful in a Jesuit liberal arts academic environment.

In 2015, I met with Mayor Emmanuel's education adviser, Arnie Rivera, and he suggested that I visit Sullivan High School, a public high school in Rogers Park, near Loyola University's Lakeshore campus. There I spoke with a very progressive principal who was delighted to learn about Arrupe College. The principal introduced me to one of his seniors, Khalil. Khalil has been an outstanding leader at and advocate for Arrupe. He has returned to Sullivan to talk about Arrupe, and Sullivan has become a top feeder school for us, along with Gary Comer, another school with high African American enrollment. Nine more of our students are coming from Solario, eight from Chicago Academy, and eight from Cristo Rey St. Martin de Porres in Waukegan. I worry about the Waukegan students because of their commute to Chicago.

Our incoming class also had seven students from Cristo Rey in the first Cristo Rey High School in Chicago's Pilsen neighborhood, and six each from Thomas Kelly High School, Epic, and Josephinum—a girls' Catholic high school sponsored by the Religious of the Sacred Heart. We enrolled five apiece from Rauner College Prep and Golder Charter Schools. Our incoming students hail from very diverse schools throughout Chicago.

It's very exciting to think about these young students joining us. We want to yield 180 students for our second year, so we will continue to recruit, and we will continue to exercise affirmative action for African American students and also for more male students. It's my experience in Jesuit higher education that the 60/40 female to male ratio is about the average. When I worked at the University of San Francisco, the gender ratios were 65/35 female to male. I think those are the numbers at Loyola University Chicago as well, so the fact that we are at 61/39 is not surprising to me.

On March 6, 2016, we had our yield event for Arrupe College, which in admissions lingo is when you have accepted your class, and it's time for them to accept you, deposit, and enroll. We call it Arrupe Night, and in 2016 we hosted about ninety students who had been accepted and their families (mothers, grandmothers, fathers, uncles, siblings). It was great to see the future of Arrupe College. The excitement of the students and their families was palpable. Two of our faculty members, Daniel Burke and Minerva Ahumada, conducted mock classes. Of course, in the spring of 2015 we didn't have faculty in place to do this, so this was a first, and it went over quite well. Minerva taught philosophy, and Daniel conducted a writing class. The newly accepted students buzzed with enthusiasm as they anticipated their classes at Arrupe.

We have incorporated a tradition I picked up from Regis University in Denver, where I serve on the board of trustees, at Arrupe Night. I had the last word, at our evening, and I informed the students about a special gift for them. "More than a thousand students applied, and you were accepted. You should feel great about yourselves." I elaborated, "We have over one hundred on the wait list, but you're in!" Then I distributed picture frames to each of the students and explained: "Look at this frame. You can put whatever picture of yourself in it that you prefer—a selfie or a picture from prom or high school graduation. But two years from now you're going to take that picture of yourself out and you're going to replace it with your diploma, your diploma from Arrupe College at Loyola University Chicago." Then I concluded, "I look forward to handing you your diploma at graduation."

Arrupe Night and all of this attention to detail is part of what I call wooing. We're wooing these students. So often other educational institutions woo those who can pay in full; or those who have 4.0s and top ACT scores; or the top athletes, artists, musicians, and so on. Our students are not being wooed by other institutions. That doesn't mean they aren't worth wooing. We want our students to feel wanted. We want them to know that we value them.

Everyone, particularly the parents, was enthusiastic, and the room erupted into cheers and applause. This reaction solidifies just how meaningful this opportunity is for our students and their families. The attendees at Arrupe Night would soon be students working toward a very concrete goal, earning that diploma to be displayed within their shiny new frames.

As families were streaming out holding their frames, sharing how excited they were to begin, a couple of students, one who was on the wait list and one who never had completed the application, were imploring Isabel to reconsider them. I took that as a sign that the event was a success.

In addition to the frames, another strategy of mine is to sign the acceptance letters for next year's incoming class, in this case, the class of 2018. I also included a handwritten message thanking those who came to Arrupe Night, for example, "Finish strong at Sullivan High School, and then get ready for Arrupe!" I always include the student's name in my handwritten message. Call me crazy. It's a large time investment on my part, but I think that it's another opportunity to woo these students by showing them that we want them to join us here, and we're invested in them and in their success with us.

Grieving

*I want to thank Arrupe for the calls and concern about the
shooting of my brother. You guys asked if I needed anything. I
ask that we don't talk about it. Going to school is my way of
getting away from things. I am grateful for Arrupe, but I have
enough on my plate.*

—Arrupe student

On Monday, April 11, 2016, in the midst of meetings, a
number of things hit my desk that reminded me of just
how volatile so many of our students' life situations are.

First, I became aware that one of our students, Edie, was contending with a legal situation. Her grandfather had died a few
months earlier. Not only had she lost her father figure, but she
had to come up with a way to pay for his funeral because she
said she could not count on anyone else in her family to help.
It turned out that her grandfather had a little checking account
that he left to Edie, but her brother gained access to the funds
and was draining the account. Hearing this, I was reminded
that after a career panel we hosted the previous week one of
the presenters, a lawyer, offered to help us going forward. So I
called him and asked him to assist Edie.

The second situation was even more dire. Yolanda informed
me that another of our students, LaDonna, had attempted suicide
after being kicked out of her family's house. LaDonna suffered
from depression already, and when she found herself homeless,
she felt helpless enough to attempt to overdose on pills. She was
hospitalized and recovering. We reached out to Mercy Home
immediately for placement.

A third student, Jorge, had been thriving at Arrupe both academically and socially. His entire life's trajectory was upended when his older brother was in the wrong place at the wrong time. The brother was shot and killed instantly. Jorge was trying to keep it together for his family. I attended the wake. His family had no resources, and they raised the money to cover the expenses of the wake and the funeral for Jorge's brother by posting their need on a GoFundMe page. Jorge expressed concern for his mother, father, and older sister. Jorge had been a fixture on the dean's list earlier that year, but he dropped off. He apologized to me for his grades slipping. "Jorge, you have a lot going on," I said. "The fact that you're here after the terrible loss that your family has experienced is remarkable to me. How can we help you?"

In the weeks previous to these episodes several friends of mine, Jesuits and laypeople, had experienced the death of parents. One friend lost her mother after a long illness. Another lost his mother after a shorter illness. I lost my father in November 2014; my mother is in her late eighties and frail. My contemporaries and I are all of the age when these things happen. The main lesson I try to share with my friends when these tragedies befall us is that while it's easy to dive back into work and family and so many other things, it is very important to grieve and to process loss. I admit that I did not do this when my father died. I flew back East and presided at his funeral and greeted all of the mourners and was touched by that and by so many people who made donations to Arrupe College in memory of my father. And then I returned to work at Arrupe and powered through it. That was not good for my interior life, and I'm becoming more and more aware of how I should have paid better attention to that and taken better care of myself.

But for Jorge, losing his brother so unexpectedly to gun violence is an entirely different experience. Losing an older parent is an event most people expect to endure, but Jorge's experience is a rupture of another kind, as are the other situations I have described. It is overwhelming at times to accompany our students both inside and outside of the classroom. It is also a privilege.

Behold Thy Son

It seems to me that obliviousness about white advantage, like obliviousness about male advantage, is kept strongly inculturated in the United States so as to maintain the myth of meritocracy, the myth that democratic choice is equally available to all. Keeping most people unaware that freedom of confident action is there for just a small number of people props up those in power and serves to keep power in the hands of the same groups that have most of it already.
—PEGGY MCINTOSH, *White Privilege*

When I go into a room where there are only white people," one of our students told his philosophy professor, "I immediately feel dumber."

That student, Juanito, loves and admires his mother, who works as a maid in a hotel downtown. She has a very challenging life. During a meeting last year Juanito told me a little about her, and he didn't play up the pathos about how hard his mother works. Rather, and his eyes told the story, he explained how much he loves and admires his mother. He continued to describe how much he hopes that with his degree from Arrupe College and whatever else he does he can begin to help his mother and decrease the pressure and burden in her life so she can enjoy a better life.

I was moved by this student's generosity. I wanted to meet Juanito's mother, to say congratulations, felicidades, you have done a great job with your son. Because our culture doesn't always recognize the valor and sacrifice of people like Juanito's mother, it can be a challenge for them to recognize their own value. Our challenge at Arrupe is to accompany Juanito into a room filled with white people and ensure not only that he does not feel dumb, but also that he belongs, that he is a valuable, valued person. My experience at Arrupe is better because of Juanito's goodness. More should have that experience, if they are open to him.

Have a Safe Weekend

For all the things that make Chicago great, for all the things that make us proud to call ourselves Chicagoans, the violence that is happening corrodes our core. It is not the Chicago we know, and it is not the Chicago we love.
—MAYOR RAHM EMMANUEL

Just before the Fourth of July weekend in 2016 our students were in class in the midst of the summer session: courses in statistics, political science, psychology, theology, philosophy, computer science, information systems, and microeconomics. The weather was beautiful, sunny but not too humid—Chicago at its best. As students were exiting Maguire Hall for the long holiday weekend, one of them, Edie, said to me, "Hey Father, you have a safe weekend." Have a safe weekend. Her wish was not for me to have a relaxing or a fun weekend, but a safe weekend.

Edie's wish for me reflects where Chicago is as a city. Homicides were up by 62 percent in 2016 from the year before. By July 4, there had already been over 1,971 shooting victims, well on pace to surpass the previous year's total of 2,988 shooting victims. The most recent victims had come from the Chicago neighborhoods of Austin, North Lawndale, South Shore, Wood-lawn, Englewood, Gage Park, Chatham, Auburn-Gresham, and West Town. These are our students' neighborhoods, where they live, and where they went to high school.

I had traveled the month before to New York for the ordinations of new Jesuit priests from my home province. It was wonderful to be back, and I was aware of how supportive the Society of Jesus is of Arrupe College, because a number of my brother Jesuits and friends greeted me with great enthusiasm and asked about my work. And then they inquired about Chicago. An article splashed on the front page of the New York Times over Memorial Day weekend had compared Chicago murder rates to those in Los Angeles and New York. In LA and New York the homicide rates have been on the decline for the past several years; in Chicago they've been on the rise since 2014. The authors of the article attributed the rise in homicides to the following:

1. Chicagoans have greater access to guns. Even though there are strict gun controls in place in Illinois, half of the guns used come from Illinois, mostly right outside of Cook County. Also, Chicago's proximity to Indiana, where the regulations are more lax, makes it easier for guns to get into the city and into the wrong hands.

2. Social media's effect on gang activity. Someone posts an item—a challenge, a piece of gossip, a denigrating remark about another person—or sends a threatening text, or tweets something insulting. The posts and texts fuel threats and/or challenges to duel. Shooting ensues, sometimes even if the original offender isn't present.

3. Police presence. The police force is smaller in Chicago than in Los Angeles or New York. Per capita, there are fewer police officers working the streets. Part of it is because the Chicago and the State of Illinois budget crises prevent them from hiring more civil servants.

4. Segregation. It is rare in New York City for 100 percent of the population in a particular neighborhood to be one ethnic group. In Chicago, particularly on the south and

west sides, that is much more common, and the group is either African American or Latino, groups that have been traditionally underserved and that have experienced the toxins of segregation and racial prejudice. I witness this when I visit our students or when I travel through their neighborhoods. I'm very aware of the meaning behind expressions like "job deserts," or "food deserts." In many of those neighborhoods where the homicide rates are so high, there are not any grocery stores, and it doesn't look like there are very many employment activities.

How does this play out at Arrupe College, besides Edie's admonition to me to be safe on the holiday weekend? When we first launched Arrupe College and were registering students for their cohorts (morning or afternoon), I presumed that college students would be more interested in the afternoon classes. I was wrong. One reason is that many of our students are uncomfortable traveling back to their neighborhoods at night. I also received several requests from students to carry mace, because when they get off the El, they feel unsafe.

Sometimes carrying mace isn't protection enough. Jennie, Yolanda, and I met with students who risk losing their financial aid unless they improve their GPAs. We asked one such student, Alberto, what had happened, why his grades had dropped. He said very matter of factly, "My best friend was shot. He's gone. I can't concentrate."

I was concerned for Alberto. I'm concerned for all of our students.

I also found myself concerned about an incoming student named John. I met John when he interviewed with us in early 2016. John and his family also attended Arrupe Night. Shortly thereafter, on a spring day, John was hanging out with his cousin on the cousin's front porch. Both John and his cousin were gunned down at 1:45 in the afternoon. John's cousin died. John, who is eighteen, survived and is now a paraplegic.

I visited John when he was at the rehab center one Sunday after mass. His girlfriend and an aunt were also there. I shook John's hand. A great grip. We talked for a while. I wanted to support John, to listen to him, and to communicate that he could start at Arrupe when he's ready. "I want you to know," I explained, "if you're ready to begin with us in August, the beginning of your freshman year, great. If for some reason you need more time for rehab or for other adjustment or transition issues, we will keep your seat for you."

John responded by saying, "Hey, Father, you said to us at Arrupe Night that over one thousand people applied to get into my class and there were only 180 seats. Aren't you going to go to your wait list?" Hmm, I thought, John is following the numbers of our story—he has the makings of a good admissions officer. My goal during that visit was to assure John and to give him some confidence and some predictability, something to look forward to, something to hope for. "John, we may go to the wait list," I said, "but not for your seat. Your seat at Arrupe has your name on it for as long as it takes you." He looked confused—and relieved.

Later in our conversation John declared that he felt that he could only attend Arrupe College for one year. "John, you know that Arrupe College is a two-year program, right?" I said. "You'll earn your associate's degree in two years with no debt, and then you can transfer to a four-year program." But John had something else on his mind. "Father," he said, "that's great, but I have a little brother, and I need to get him out of Chicago." I looked at John and asked him very simply, "Is your brother hanging with the wrong crowd?" His brother is twelve. "It's not that, at least not yet," John responded, "but my brother loves guns."

I was very direct with John when I asked, "Has your brother put it together what a gun has done to you?" John paused and said, "He's like how I was—he thinks he's invincible."

John's whole life had changed, and yet he was concerned about his little brother. I told John how impressed I was with his generosity toward his brother, but I also said: "You know you have a lot going on right now. Let's focus on your rehab, on your getting better and learning how to live life in a new way, on coming to Arrupe and adjusting to being a college student at a Jesuit university. Then, once you enroll and get into a rhythm, let's talk about your brother and your future and his future. But let's do one day at a time." That seemed to resonate.

I have visited with John a number of times since. My money is on him. I think he'll be with us, if not at orientation, then in class.

Looking back on the beginning of the Fourth of July weekend, Edie was spot on when she wished me a safe holiday. She's a daughter of Chicago and someone who, like all of our students, is learning to navigate herself and her life and her family in the midst of an upsurge in gun violence. Stay safe.

Stalemate in Springfield Leaves Students' Futures Hanging in the Balance

May you live in interesting times.
—TRADITIONAL CHINESE BLESSING/CURSE

On Tuesday, March 27, 2016, our DLG met to discuss a financial crisis. I had attended another meeing earlier that day with Loyola University's council of deans, and the interim provost, Patrick Boyle, led a discussion about the university's finances and the growing concern over what was going to happen to Illinois' Monetary Award Program (MAP), which provides grants to state residents who demonstrate financial need to attend college. At the time there was a stalemate in Springfield over the state budget, and the MAP money had not been dispersed to any institution of higher learning. For Loyola, that amounted to more than ten million dollars, $400,000 of which was designated for Arrupe students.

Our financial model is based on all of our students—except undocumented immigrants—qualifying for MAP and Pell Grants. As we anticipate at least doubling our enrollment in the future, the loss of MAP Grants would mean Arrupe College would be out at least $900,000. I had been proceeding on the premise (as had other leaders in the university) that the state would come to its senses, that the leaders would realize how critical the MAP funds were to higher education and would find the funding in the budget to make this possible. Already there was a lot of discussion of a "brain drain," how young women and men who are talented academically are leaving the state in order to pursue education elsewhere because of the lack of MAP funds. Even when we presumed that there would be no MAP funding for 2016 but that it would kick in again for fiscal year 2017, Provost Patrick Boyle told us he was beginning to believe that the MAP situation was permanent.

Pat's words transported me back in time. I haven't seen this movie in thirty years, but in Moonstruck, when Loretta (the character played by Cher) slaps Johnny (played by Nicolas Cage), she yells, "Snap out of it!" I felt as though someone, maybe Pat Boyle, was slapping me into reality and saying, "Snap out of it. The MAP funds are not going to be available, and you need a Plan B." While our colleagues across campus were asked to examine efficiencies and consequent budget cuts, those of us at Arrupe knew we needed to emphasize fundraising. We are growing a program that is not yet at full enrollment and thus too new to identify cuts when we have barely completed one fiscal year in operation. Before I left the deans' meeting, I conferred with David Prasse, the vice provost for academic and faculty resources, and asked him for talking points. "What am I supposed to tell people about our financial model here as stakeholders connect the dots and recognize that the MAP money is going away?" I asked. "And what do Derrick and Isabel tell our feeder schools and prospective students that they are recruiting?" David shook his head and said, "Steve, right now we are preparing all of our financial packages presuming that there will be MAP money. We are committed to your students." That's the message I delivered to the DLG.

I deeply appreciate Loyola University's commitment to Arrupe College and to our students. This is a signature program for Loyola. It's also significant for Chicago and for Jesuit higher education. That said, the situation in Springfield was very troubling for everyone. I looked at Maggie and wondered: where is the money going to come from? When we reach our full enrollment of four hundred, which I anticipated we would reach in another two years given the robust applicant pools we had already experienced, we would eventually need to raise $1.6 million to offset what we weren't getting from the state. That is doable, but certainly not what we expected to raise. For the average student, MAP money comes to thirty-seven hundred dollars a year; that's a deal breaker for our students, who have expected family contributions of under six thousand dollars a year. Preparing a financial Plan B proved to be very stressful.

At the time of this writing I felt we were beginning to gain some traction, but not enough. The McCormick Foundation gift was extraordinary. A lot of my friends in New York, Washington DC, and California had given seed money, and we've collaborated well with Loyola's foundations department, who've helped us to identify and to prepare grant proposals to other foundations. But as Angela Liegel, one of my colleagues in development, said, we are still the new game in town. Once there's another new exciting story in higher education, we could be left out in the cold. So my concern is to develop a culture of philanthropy for

Arrupe that is heavily dependent upon a Chicago-based donor-ship—men and women who are supportive of us and excited about what we're trying to accomplish and who will contribute to an annual fund. This is unlike what I've experienced before in fundraising, most recently at Loyola School in New York, where we had an established alumni base and a current parent base. That is not our situation at Arrupe.

We are also part of a larger question about the future of Chicago and of Illinois. To be successful economically in the future, both the state and the city need citizens who are well educated, who can contribute to civic life and progress, and who have the intellectual capital to exercise leadership. Chicago is a great city that offers much, but the economic crisis is an ominous portent.

On Easter Monday, March 28, 2016, I attended a Chicago City Club luncheon where our speakers were from the United Way, Access Living, and Metropolitan Family Services. The topic was "The Impact of the Illinois State Budget Impasse on Human Services." I'm new to Illinois, but I'm finding out that the stalemate in Springfield has wreaked havoc in areas most of us never considered. These presenters shared the following grim statistics:

- No state funding is flowing for adult education and job training services.
- Approximately eighty-four thousand seniors have lost Meals on Wheels and/or in-home community-based services.
- Senior protective services are not being funded.
- Centers for Independent Living are not being funded, resulting in cuts to training for personal assistants and referrals for those with disabilities.
- Nearly fifteen thousand young people lost access to high-quality comprehensive after-school services at 122 sites around the state.

- The state stopped funding grants for psychiatrists, forcing providers to turn away new patients with serious mental illness who do not have health insurance.
- Victims of rape, who often need immediate counseling, have to wait up to twelve weeks for appointments due to reduction of services.
- Agencies have taken on more than thirty-five million dollars in debt while they await payment from the state.
- More than four hundred million dollars in fiscal year 2016 funding will be owed to agencies by the end of June.

Terrifying. In July 2015, 34 percent of non-profits had to make budget cuts; in January 2016, 85 percent had to make cuts as a result of Springfield's impasse. Many programs have been cut by more than 20 percent, affecting children and working adults the most. Forty-nine percent of agencies have already tapped into their cash reserves. Agencies have taken on more than thirty-five million dollars of debt to stay open; 27 percent of agencies have laid off staff. This is a terrible terrain in which to be working.

Nevertheless, and I may be whistling a different tune as I go deeper into my experiences here in Chicago and Illinois, in a perverse sort of way I think that this is where I'm meant to be. This is a very difficult environment, but it is where the greatest need is. As a Jesuit I have desired to work with a tough population; the population here has so many disadvantages financially, and the environment here is so volatile, but our students are extraordinary young women and men. The situation reminds me of Pedro Arrupe's great line—"More than ever I find myself in the hands of God."

There's no cushion in Illinois. There is less and less of a cushion in higher education. Loyola University Chicago is better off than many, but this can't last forever. So for me, there is a strong sense of entering into the lives of the materially poor, of uncertainty, and of seeing diminishment. I recognize that even if this is where I am called to be, it may also truly become one of the greatest professional, pastoral, and personal challenges of my life.

The Issue of MAP Funding at Arrupe College

Today we are truly a global family. What happens in one part of the world may affect us all. . . . As interdependents, therefore, we have no other choice than to develop what I call a sense of universal responsibility.

—The Dalai Lama

The MAP crisis resulted in phone calls and emails from Loyola University's student newspaper. Reporters asked questions like, Will Arrupe College be able to maintain itself without MAP money? What is the future for the students and faculty if Arrupe College is not continued? While I recognize that MAP is an important part of our budget, part of our financial model, I began to wonder why these questions aren't being posed to my peers, the other deans at Loyola University? The uncertainty about MAP is a concern for all higher education institutions in Illinois, not solely Arrupe College. And yet the focus was placed on us. When I spoke to reporters, I tried to be patient. "Your story is about the twenty-four hundred plus Loyola University students who qualify for MAP, not just the 110 Arrupe students within that larger number. That's a much bigger story in terms of impact." And yet the spotlight on Arrupe continued. Will Arrupe be able to stay open? What will happen to Arrupe? Loyola's student newspaper had Arrupe closing before we completed our first year.

My patience was exhausted when I read the student newspaper article about the MAP situation—a story exclusively about Arrupe. At one point in the story a Loyola administrator was quoted as saying, "Without MAP, Arrupe is unsustainable." I was livid. I contacted him immediately. "How am I supposed to recruit students, hire faculty and staff, and raise money when the newspaper quotes you saying we are unsustainable?"

Despite the strange focus on Arrupe, when Loyola University asked me to send students to a MAP rally in Springfield, I consented. Arrupe students would be joining their classmates from Loyola to influence by their presence the political discourse. I spoke with a friend who is president of a Catholic college in Illinois with a much smaller enrollment than Loyola. That college sent 170 undergrads to the Springfield rally. Loyola was represented by six students: five enrolled at Arrupe, and one from outside of Arrupe. Six out of more than twenty-four hundred Loyola students who qualified for MAP.

I contacted the editor of Loyola's student newspaper. "I have a story for you," I said. I submitted the following to the editorial staff.

Inclusion in light of MAP Funding

Dear Editorial Staff of the Loyola PHOENIX:

Last week, I attended a panel discussion sponsored by the Association of Governing Boards entitled "Toward an inclusive campus community." Designed for trustees of private and public postsecondary institutions, the panel consisted of leaders in higher education who also are women and men of color. Among the panelists were the interim president of the University of Missouri (Mizzou), the president of Morehouse College, and a trustee at the Ohio State University.

The panelists candidly shared their perspectives on how diversity falls short. "We admit students of color," observed one, "and we celebrate. Then what?" "We become enraptured with our enrollment statistics," said another panelist, "but we don't pay attention to the inclusion of our students." Trustees who attended the presentation were encouraged "to understand what inclusion is: when a student can say about his or her college, 'I belong here.'"

At Arrupe, Loyola University Chicago's newest college, my colleagues and I have focused on accompanying our students as they grow in their appreciations that they belong at a private, Jesuit, Catholic, liberal arts college. University of Texas researcher David Yeager states that students are at the highest risk of dropping out of school if they feel like they don't belong; in addition, Yeager cites research that indicates for first generation students from low income backgrounds, achieving a sense of belonging in higher ed is especially challenging.

Arrupe College would not exist were it not a part of Loyola University Chicago. Colleagues across campus have collaborated with us as we faced accreditation, created a brand, built the curriculum, and hired faculty and staff. The results: 91% retention of our inaugural class so far, and more than 1,000 young women and men currently completing senior year in Chicago's public, Catholic, and charter high schools, have applied for the 180 seats in next year's freshmen class.

Arrupe students are enjoying success because they feel that they belong at Loyola. One Arrupe student recently informed a member of the U.S. congress who was visiting our college, "I see myself as a Loyola student." Last Saturday, as I walked through the Damen Student Center, I was delighted to bump into three Arrupe students working on their intro to stats class together.

These students can belong because they are eligible for Pell and MAP grants. They can belong because much of Arrupe's overhead, in Maguire Hall at LUC's Water Tower Campus, including utilities, technology support, and security is absorbed by the university. They would not otherwise experience a Jesuit education and have the opportunity to attend a college at Loyola for two years and earn an associate's degree at minimal costs.

The budget impasse in Springfield, despite the recent partial funding approval, has impacted more than 2,400 Loyola students, 110 of whom are Arrupe students eligible for MAP grants. Indeed, Arrupe students, like many fellow Loyola students, depend on MAP, Pell and other aid to complete their education. Why, then, do the reporters of this paper focus on Arrupe students and Arrupe College when the impasse affects so many Loyola and other Illinois college students? The uncertainty about MAP is an Illinois higher education problem and yet the focus is disproportionately placed on Arrupe, where 97% of our students are women and men of color.

If inclusion in higher ed is defined as a student being able to say, "I belong here" at a college or university, we at Arrupe are receiving a mixed message. The MAP problem is a major issue affecting Loyola University and all other schools in Illinois. Please don't single us out. Arrupe is part of, not separate from the rest of Loyola University Chicago, where all of our students "belong."

The newspaper printed my piece. "My mother used to say, 'Don't be a bad influence,'" I said to the editor. "You've been a bad influence about the MAP story. By making MAP a problem for black and Hispanic students at Arrupe, Loyola University Chicago missed the opportunity to be a stronger presence in Springfield. Don't you get it? 'We' is much more powerful than 'you' or 'me.'" Arrupe hasn't received any more interview requests about MAP.

A Day in the Life of the Dean
of Arrupe College

If there is no struggle, there is no progress.
—Frederick Douglass

Monday, May 16, 2016, was the first full day of my annual retreat. Anyone who knows a Jesuit knows that doing an eight-day silent retreat is an important part of Jesuit life. I went on my retreat this year with my friend and fellow Jesuit Fr. Jim Prehn. Jim is the superior of the community at Loyola University and has been very supportive of Arrupe College; he serves on our admissions committee and has agreed to teach a course for us during our summer session.

More on my retreat experiences during the first year of Arrupe College later. On the last day of classes before my retreat I had a visit from a potential donor named Tim. He is an acquaintance of one of our board members, Luis Gutierrez, and he was no pushover. He asked a lot of tough questions about Arrupe College, our financial model and our outcomes. I hope I presented Arrupe well. That said, as always, it was our students who won Tim over. While we toured the building, Tim met a student named Socorro, who was reading for her philosophy course in metaphysics. Philosophy has been a foundation of Jesuit education, of Catholic education, and this impressed Tim, who is a very active Catholic. Socorro herself impressed him, too. As Tim was leaving, we bumped into another student named Donetia, who, truth be told, began the year with an almost surly attitude. Over the last several months she had become much more engaged. I said to her, "Now, Donetia, you're leaving for a three-week break before summer session begins. We're going to see you back here, right?" She replied in front of Tim: "There is no way that I'm going to stop. No one can stop me. I'm not stopping. I'm pursuing my degree." Donetia's delivery was very genuine and very animated. Tim and I said goodbye in Arrupe's lobby, but before he left, Tim assured me that he would support Arrupe. I assured Tim that I would contact him after I returned from retreat.

After I said goodbye to Tim, I hopped into a cab and headed down to the Union League Club, where I had been able to put together a lunch with Arne Duncan, who recently had concluded his service in the Obama administration as the Secretary of Education; Rob Martin, the chair of the board at Cristo Rey; Tony Ortiz, the president of Cristo Rey; and Joe Seminetta, our board chair. We had an opportunity to talk to Arne about the work and the students at Cristo Rey and at Arrupe College. He seemed very engaged. Also, we learned about his new work providing job-skills training for young men between the ages of seventeen and twenty-four, and the problems of black-on-black crime and the lack of marketable job skills.

I explained to Arne that I just been in Washington DC at the Association of Governing Boards conference and was inspired by Patricia McGuire, the president of Trinity Washington College, who talked about how important partnerships are. Arne spoke about his own partnership with Steve Jobs's widow, Lorene Powell Jobs, and how she is helping him fund his program for African American men to get job skills that they need. Arne then committed to visiting Arrupe College later in the day. I received an email from him saying, "Thanks for the work that you are doing and the difference you are making." I'm so grateful for the opportunities that I have to represent Arrupe College, to represent our students and what we're trying to do to make a Jesuit, liberal-arts, post-secondary education available and accessible to our students. It's an honor to interact with people of the caliber and dedication of Arne Duncan.

On my way back from the luncheon I spoke with a friend of mine in New York who just had been diagnosed with cancer. This friend is a graduate of Loyola School. He is in remarkable shape. He is a young man, only forty or so, and his kids are young. His wife is composed, and his doctor diagnosed his situation early, but I told him I would be praying for him, his family, and his doctors during my retreat.

I went from that conversation to meeting with some architects about the Student Commons space we are redeveloping on the first floor of Arrupe College to serve as a dining hall and an all-purpose room. I've engaged two architects thus far, and this was the second group that came in. They really wowed us with three different alternatives that were interesting for us to see. Maggie and I met with them and also with the university's architect, Peter Schlecht.

After the architects left, we met with a new board member. One of our trustees, Rick Hammond, an attorney, introduced me several weeks ago to Derrick Blakley. He is a graduate of Hales Franciscan High School and a newscaster for Channel 2 in Chicago. Derrick can help us with our media strategy for Arrupe College. I am grateful for his expertise and for his presence on our board. I told him about what we needed in our first conversation, and he said to me, "You know, Father, you had me at hello." We are now up to twenty-one board members (including me), and I'm trying to connect with several other candidates for board membership.

From there I hosted the faculty for happy hour. We've done this at the end of each session of courses, and we usually go to the McCormick and Schmick's that is within walking distance of Arrupe College. My colleagues Julia, Andy, Daniel, and Rene were all talking about what our students call us. In my case, I'm pretty old school (or maybe I'm just pretty old at this point). They call me Fr. Katsouros or Fr. K. With some of my younger colleagues, the students are less formal, and we were talking about the pluses and minuses of that. What impresses me about Julia, Andy, Rene, and Daniel is their thoughtfulness about our students and also how well they know our students.

From there I headed to a dinner for the Magnificent Mile Association, a group of retailers on Michigan Avenue headed by John Chikow. John is very enthusiastic about Arrupe College and is trying to influence retailers to hire our students. I enjoyed meeting up with John and his wife, Vicki.

Before I left for retreat, I saw a group of our students and asked them about their upcoming breaks. One of them, Scott, asked me, "Father, do you ever take much of a break?" I said, "Not really." For me, retreats are not vacations. During a retreat I'm trying to be more attentive to God and listen to what God is asking of me more singularly than I typically have the time to do. And sometimes what God has to say takes me somewhere I had not anticipated.

Scott observed, "So you never really get a break." Then he paused, and in front of other students he said, "You know, Father, without you here, we know that we would not be here." That really moved me. I said, "I have a very strong work ethic, and what drives that ethic and what inspires that ethic is you and all of your classmates. I admire you and think so highly of you and think you're great. That's why I work the way I do, because you and Arrupe are worth it." It was pretty simple and direct but very sincere, and a powerful affirmation before my retreat began.

What Does God Hope for You?

The ministers of the gospel must be people who can warm the hearts of the people, who walk through the dark night with them, who know how to dialogue with them and to descend themselves into their people's night in the darkness without getting lost.

—POPE FRANCIS

During my retreat in May 2016 I read a great deal by and about Pope Francis. My reading included *The Great Reformer*, Austen Ivereigh's biography, as well as Mark Shriver's manuscript that became his book on the pope, *Pilgrimage*. A few things from these works struck me in relation to what I've experienced at Arrupe College.

Mark writes about a priest who knew Pope Francis in Buenos Aires. The priest said of him: "I think that what he does is get people to turn their eyes toward the poor, as he did in Buenos Aires. He got the city of Buenos Aires to look at the villas but also the places of suffering." To help out, but also to learn from them. To have more solidarity, to share, in other words, not only to go to help, but also to learn from the other, to learn from the poor. He showed them the periphery, not only so they could help but also so they could learn, learn about this human reality and learn about the difficulties that people are facing. And, in so doing, seek greater integration.

Mark then asks, What does it mean to learn from the poor? To have integration with the poor? To go out to the periphery?

That last question is one that I like quite a bit, because I find that so often at Arrupe College we are learning from our students, from what our students are bringing to their classes and to the college. They have been on the periphery of higher education, of Jesuit education, of private college education. Working with them through the experiences they're having, the difficulties they're facing, both helps us to bring them to greater integration and helps us understand the reality of their lives.

A reporter who was very enthusiastic about doing a national story about Arrupe College visited us. She met with Mike Garanzini and with me. In my conversation with her I talked about some of the students she wanted to interview. One student had been homeless, so she wanted to explore that student's daily struggle to find shelter. Two other students were undocumented. One of them had seen his brother shot and killed the month before.

I told this reporter's contact at Loyola University Chicago's marketing and communications office that the article she was proposing felt sensationalistic and exploitative. We had only recently found housing for the homeless student, and it wasn't like her homelessness had been years ago and she'd had time to work through those issues. It was raw. The student who had lost his brother was merely weeks removed from that tragedy. And undocumented students are often uncomfortable talking about their status because they live in the shadows; they are afraid that they or members of their families might be discovered and deported.

I knew my resistance frustrated the reporter and the university, but I worried about the students. I found in Pope Francis's strategies of going to the peripheries a healthier and more reassuring model in terms of learning from our students and talking about how they've been on the periphery of higher education, but also reminding them that the whole point of Arrupe College is to see what they have to contribute and to learn from them.

It also struck me in reading Ivereigh's *The Great Reformer* that Pope Francis is very interested in inculturation. Ivereigh notes that Francis considers inculturation to be a model for missionaries and pastors who need to recognize the inherent dignity of every culture and to become enmeshed with it. Such a degree of inculturation, Francis wrote when still archbishop of Buenos Aires, was costly, especially for Jesuits who might be suddenly called to another mission and therefore must go through the process again. "When he is moved, he feels pain," says Bergoglio. "If it doesn't hurt, he's not a Jesuit."

That statement lingered with me for a while on my retreat. In just five years I had moved from New York City, where I'd spent most of my life, to San Francisco, and then to Chicago. I don't want to overemphasize the point—it's not like I'm living and working in Somalia or some other place with constant emergency needs—but still, these moves come at a cost as I had to reconstruct my life again and again and develop new contacts and learn new cultures. Every time, I needed to embrace my new assignment as I mourned my last one.

The major reason I was able to embrace my assignment to Arrupe College fully is because of the students and because of the school's mission. Those students and that mission, I am able to say, are worth the pain that Bergoglio acknowledges occurs for Jesuits when they are reassigned, when they move, when they say goodbye to an apostolate, to a work, to a community they love, and move on to a new assignment. While I have experienced the pain about which Bergoglio writes, I find the work at Arrupe College so compelling, and our students so worthwhile, so worthy of this chapter of my life.

Another insight from Ivereigh's book was that Bergoglio did not believe that the clergy or the bishops or Rome were in possession of the truth and then distributed it downward, but that the Holy Spirit was revealed through a dialogue between the faithful people and the universal church. This radical stance, this option for ordinary people, is exemplified by the way God is revealed in Jesus Christ two thousand years ago to the fishermen and the shepherds of the Holy Land. I recognized that my situation at Arrupe was a good example of Bergoglio's belief—I certainly feel as though the Holy Spirit is being revealed to me in the students at Arrupe College, ordinary students who I think are really quite extraordinary.

Another quote from Bergoglio that struck me had to do with the realities of ministry: "The ministers of the gospel must be people who can warm the hearts of the people, who walk through the dark night with them, who know how to dialogue with them and to descend themselves into their people's night in the darkness without getting lost." I try not to talk about seeing myself in the students of Arrupe College, because I recognize that I am older and that I come from an entirely different background. Yes, I was the first member of my family to go to college, but it's different. Not better or worse, just different. Nevertheless, I do treasure my opportunity to walk with the students and dialogue with them. I like to think that I warm their hearts on occasion and at times descend into their nights. I also hope the flip side is true, that I can celebrate with them who they are and their accomplishments and this journey that we're undertaking at Arrupe College.

One final quote from Ivereigh's book affected my time on retreat:

> Bergoglio insisted that the Jesuits were not going to teach but were going to be taught by the *pueblo fiel* [faithful people]. The Jesuits' capacity for inserting themselves into the culture they were sent into to evangelize was "the decisive test" of their faith. "How difficult it is and how lonely it can feel when I realize that I must learn from the people their language, their terms of reference, their values, not as a way of polishing my theology but as a way of being that transforms me."

My experience at Arrupe College has been transformative for the students, for my colleagues, and for me.

During my retreat I checked in with a good friend and former spiritual director, Jane Ferdon, a Dominican sister who works at the Jesuit School of Theology in Berkeley. I met her there over twenty years ago when I participated in her spiritual direction practicum to learn to be a spiritual director. I had made arrangements to speak with Jane on the phone three times during the course of the retreat. As I was reflecting back about the year and about the launching of Arrupe College, about our students, about how our students build community, Jane interrupted and asked, "Steve, what does God hope for you?"

It was typical Jane—she was concerned for me, concerned I was working too hard. Along with that important reminder, I also was reminded of a recommendation by an Indian Jesuit, Anthony DeMello, a spiritual guru in many ways. DeMello suggests in his books the following spiritual exercise: behold God beholding you smiling. Jane and DeMello both were getting at the same thing: try to imagine God's perspective. Imagine what it's like to see yourself through God's lens. What does God hope for you?

Those simple reminders to try to step outside myself and see myself in God's loving gaze reminded me of a gospel passage I had preached on earlier in the spring. "I have much more to tell you, but you cannot bear it now; the Spirit will guide you" (John 16:12–13). Around that time, I was struggling with several difficult situations, including two close friends who had been diagnosed with cancer. I was trying to offer support both through phone calls and email. Another situation much on my mind was that of John, our student who had been shot a few weeks earlier and left paralyzed. I knew I would be meeting soon with his family, and I was anticipating that visit.

I thought back to that gospel passage. Jesus had not told the disciples everything they must know. So, too, when I was talking to my friends dealing with serious illness, or John and his family, the wisdom that I have—being a Jesuit, being a priest, being a fellow traveler, being a companion, being fifty-six years old—is a gradual wisdom, a wisdom based on a process. And a wisdom based on the Spirit, the Spirit that continues to extend the revelation of Jesus. We are works in progress, works in the progress of the revelation of Jesus. I know that revelation is based on Jesus, is grounded in his ministry, but according to Jesus, according to John's Gospel, the Spirit is continuing to unfold what revelation means after the departure of Jesus. Revelation is extended. Revelation is present in the here and now.

I preached on that gospel on the Feast of the Holy Trinity. It's a heady topic, the Trinity, and rare is the theologian or preacher who can communicate the mystery of it in a way that makes sense to the people in the pews during a seven-minute homily. My own style, of course, is to make it concrete, so for me, the Trinity becomes alive and well in the community that I know, that I'm in right now—in this case, at Arrupe College.

A number of our Arrupe students during the session of classes right before my retreat had been taking statistics, so I shared with the students that when I was an undergrad, I struggled mightily with the subject. It wasn't until I was a doctoral student that statistics finally made sense to me. While I doubt that telling eighteen-year-olds that statistics finally came alive for me when I was getting my doctorate was exactly a consolation to them, it did help me to approximate this notion of ongoing revelation, this idea that our knowledge of ourselves and God and creation and history is gradual, that it's a process, rather than a eureka or thunderclap moment.

I had found a more concrete example of this gradual process of revelation a few weeks before, in a moment I've mentioned before, when I bumped into three of our students at the Lake Shore Campus of Loyola University. Dalia was the guide, because she really likes the subject matter and understands it. I could not yet say the same about Jamal and Mike, but I could see that they were growing in their appreciation. They were works in progress. It was a gradual process for them.

Jesus tells the disciples, "I have much to tell you but you cannot bear it now. The Spirit will guide you." So, too, Dalia was guiding Jamal and Mike. Jane has been guiding me. Dalia and Jane were vehicles of the Spirit for us.

As I travel deeper into the community of Arrupe College, I want to make sure I'm listening to Dalia and Mike and Jamal and the other students and their experiences, rather than imposing what I think they need. We're all limited; we're all works in progress. But Jesus tells us that our limitations are surmountable, that the Holy Spirit will guide us if we allow ourselves to be led. And so for me, leadership means allowing myself to be led at times, particularly by our students and by my colleagues.

Jane's question was not one just for my annual retreat, but one that I knew I needed to let guide me in the days and weeks and months ahead—What does God hope for you, Steve? I think that what God hopes for me has to do with community, like the community of the Trinity and the communities I participate in and am a part of in my day-to-day life. I think what God hopes for me is a network of relationships that guide me closer to God and to a greater understanding of God. And maybe all that will guide me to Tony DeMello's insight: *Behold God beholding you and smiling.*

Strengths, Weaknesses, Opportunities, and Threats

Every weakness contains within itself a strength.
—Shūsaku Endō

On Wednesday July 13, 2016, the faculty and staff of Arrupe College gathered at Loyola University Chicago's Lake

Shore Campus for an offsite retreat. On our to-do list was a SWOT analysis. Anyone who has worked in a large organization is probably familiar with this activity: a thorough multifaceted review of the organization's strengths, weaknesses, opportunities, and threats.

In some ways the timing of this could not have been better, because no sooner had I had announced we were going to do this exercise than I received an email from the provost's office asking that I submit a SWOT analysis for Loyola University Chicago's incoming president, Dr. Jo Ann Rooney. So this was an opportunity for me to gather information from my colleagues at Arrupe to be able to offer Jo Ann a report that was not solely through my lens and my experience.

I made my usual pitch to my colleagues that St. Ignatius Loyola always calls us to be contemplatives in action, and while most of us have the action part down, the contemplative part is harder—we don't make the time, we don't have the time. So it was good to yank ourselves out of Maguire Hall and Loyola University Chicago's Water Tower Campus, and go off together to engage in contemplation. It was on a Wednesday, so there were no classes and everyone was able to be a part of the discussion. We began with an "Examen," a reflection of our experiences of the entire year. I asked my colleagues to identify our big wins from the year.

That conversation naturally segued into our analysis of our *strengths*. First of all, we realized that we are a flexible and collegial culture. When we recognized that five eight-week sessions were not working for our students, that for most of our students, the sessions were too short, we relied on our faculty's early observations of our students. Based on those observations, as well as our shared desire to meet our students where they were and to provide them with the best post-secondary higher education experience possible, we agreed to shift to a schedule of two semesters and one summer session. We wanted to hold on to the idea from our original vision of Arrupe College that our students stay enrolled in classes year round, because the research shows that when students are on long breaks from classes they usually lose two to three months of progress in math and reading. We were able to adjust our semester schedules and be flexible when the data suggested it was needed.

Another strength is that we are ambitious. Our desire for an 85 percent retention rate and for an average GPA of 2.85 is evidence of our very high expectations. We don't want to "dumb it down" for our students. Oftentimes our students have suffered from having very low expectations set for them; we have found if we ask a lot from them, they often meet or exceed our expectations.

Second, we engage in a lot of problem solving. One reason for this is our belief in *cura personalis*, care of the whole person, and meeting students where they're at, being aware of their backgrounds and their needs. Let me give an example. One Friday afternoon just before our SWOT analysis, I found myself at Pearl Vision with Gisselle, one of our dean's list students. Gisselle had lost her glasses, and Medicaid wouldn't pay for a new pair until August. But we were in the middle of our summer session, and Gisselle was enrolled in a statistics class. She couldn't see the numbers and was frustrated. Finally I said, "The heck with it. Let's get a cab." And Gisselle and I went to buy her glasses. When Gisselle found out that Arrupe College was paying for the glasses, she started crying. But our goal wasn't just to make Gisselle feel wanted; we wanted Gisselle to be successful. If she couldn't see the numbers, she couldn't be successful.

Another reason we are good at problem solving is our use of metrics. For example, we kept very close track of students who did well during our first summer session in terms of improving their attendance and also their GPA. We promised those students that when it is time for college tours, they would be the first ones to go—a terrific incentive. By tracking improvement—not just overall performance—we were able to inspire some of our students to reach a little higher academically.

Another strength I am grateful for is that we are part of Loyola University Chicago. We occupy a great building and a great location for commuters, and it is very meaningful for our students to be part of a university that has been in Chicago since 1870.

Finally, we offer innovative teaching, advising, and student support. We offer an unusual level of support for further college placement; we want to have a plan for every student once he or she completes a two-year associate's degree at Arrupe College.

Harder to acknowledge but just as important to recognize are our *weaknesses.* First and foremost, a number of my colleagues said that we need a better flow of information. They were talking about better use of the website, but I could also see numerous instances when we were all going rogue.

Another weakness is that our block schedule leaves limited time for student meetings and extracurriculars. Our students are in a morning session or an afternoon session for three hours, with only 1:00–2:00 p.m. free for meetings for student government, for meals, for tutoring. While some students are able to come in before 9:45 a.m. or stay after 5:15 p.m. to take part in meals and activities, others are not. For the future we are interested in getting feedback on best practices from other educational institutions. It may just be a fact that this is as good as it gets in a commuter school

Beginning without a social worker was a weakness that we remedied in November.

Our relationship with Loyola University Chicago is another weakness, although paradoxically it is also listed as a strength. It can be challenging to be entrepreneurial within the traditional pace and culture of higher education. Loyola University Chicago has been revolutionary in initiating Arrupe, but decision making on the university level often does not match the need to move quickly to seize or optimize an opportunity.

As for opportunities, key is the chance to work with partner organizations and networks that have demonstrated enormous interest and goodwill in what we are attempting at Arrupe.

One obvious example is the Association of Jesuit Colleges and Universities network, which is very supportive of our work and our future plans. We're also seeing a lot of opportunity to collaborate with local non-profits. For example, a few days before our SWOT analysis, our leadership team met with leaders from Year Up, a group that helps young people develop "soft skills" that will lead to a job. When I look at our students, I recognize that not all of them will transition to a four-year institution; what are we going to do with and for these students? They will need to enter the workforce upon graduation, and groups like Year Up might be a good option for some of them.

One unexpected opportunity we have discovered is our chance to grow our brand, emphasizing care of our students and our retention rate. While sometimes we all worry that being described as affordable can be stigmatizing in the world of higher education, many other stakeholders in the educational realm are concerned about the cost of higher education. They worry that tuition costs make higher education less accessible and less achievable for anyone from a low-income background. Using our model elsewhere, even nationally, should be an ongoing conversation in the future. We feel that our brand is less about "we serve the poor" than it is about an emphasis on how we care for our students—there's that *cura personalis* again!— and our ability to keep the retention of students high, even when challenged with difficult socioeconomic obstacles.

Finally, we face some significant external *threats*. One is the MAP funding difficulties. If we lose our MAP funding, we will need to raise an additional million-plus dollars, because our financial model is based on students qualifying for MAP and Pell Grants. Another related threat is that the Illinois state government seems to be broken; Springfield, the state capital, is dysfunctional.

Another obvious threat is violence in Chicago and its impact on Arrupe's students, families, and neighborhoods. Some other external threats are simply the practical obstacles to success in the underserved neighborhoods of Chicago. Several of our students are pregnant, and other students struggle with childcare. Some have family members who can watch their children while they're in classes and commuting and studying and writing papers, but others don't have that support. Similarly, we face a painful lack of housing options for Arrupe students who are homeless. We've benefited from our relationship with Mercy Home for Boys and Girls, but homelessness remains an issue; we often know of five students at a time who have nowhere to live.

On the national level we have to recognize as a threat the decisions of the US government regarding undocumented parents and the deportation of undocumented immigrants. Our undocumented students also do not qualify for Pell and MAP funding. These students make up 20 percent of our freshman class and 20 percent of our rising sophomore class. That's a lot to offset with fundraising.

Another threat in our future is a hard one to admit but is a reality; right now we are the pretty, shiny new thing in terms of foundations and fundraising. That won't last forever. People are excited about our successes and our ambitions, but our funding from foundations and individuals could be jeopardized once the next new thing comes along. Without the hard data—such as graduation rates or four-year college placement rates, we can't interest foundations that want proof on our success. We also don't want to be confused with programs like Cristo Rey High School, which are twenty years old and have more established models and metrics, when we are looking for financial and institutional partners for our ambitious goals.

Ultimately, a SWOT analysis is beneficial for both its inspirational moments and its troubling ones. It is enjoyable and uplifting to hear our strengths and our opportunities, but it is also crucial that we be able to identify and try to remedy our weaknesses and the threats we face.

Jesus of Arrupe College

This work has been a labor of love, complicated and sincerely from the heart, and I hope and pray that your students will feel welcomed and affirmed.

—Janet McKenzie

In 2007, when I was still at Loyola School in New York City, generous donors there made it possible for us to renovate the school chapel. The renovation included commissioning several works of art. I had long admired the work of Janet McKenzie. Janet's art celebrates men, women, and children of all races and confronts stereotypical thinking with inclusive and luminous images. Her paintings *Jesus of the People, Epiphany, Station IV, Jesus Meets His Mother, Mary Magdalene—Invitation to Love,* and others resonate with me.

For the chapel at Loyola School I asked Janet to paint an image of the Holy Family. She sent some mockups. The first was a black woman holding a white child. I returned it to her. "Looks too much like a lot of the nannies I see pushing strollers in Central Park," I told Janet. The next iteration was a black mother and child. "We're getting there," I said. "But let's get the man involved in the childcare." The third time was the charm. The painting she did for us—*The Holy Family*—continues to grace Loyola School chapel, providing a source of meditation and reinforcing the Jesuit notion of how God is in all things—and all people.

I thought of Janet more than once when our students began their studies at Arrupe College. I reached out to her, and I sent her photos that Loyola University's photographers had taken of our students—during the summer enrichment program, at the opening with Archbishop Cupich and Mayor Emmanuel, in classes, over breakfasts and lunches. I asked Janet if she could depict Jesus as a college student—eighteen or nineteen years old—surrounded by other young people.

"The idea is simple," Janet responded in an email. "A group of beautiful and diverse students with Jesus as the central figure—some reaching out to the viewer and some within themselves." She continued, "I guess it just represents the duality of our natures, of life, the external and internal."

I spoke with friends in New York who remembered *The Holy Family* in Loyola School's chapel. They said they would fund the new painting for Arrupe College. "I will paint young, racially and gender diverse people grouped together reflecting the variety of students attending Arrupe College," Janet wrote in our agreement letter. "They will look out of the canvas to students, faculty, and visitors conveying youthful and universal feelings of longing for friendship and community." I nodded as I read Janet's words. Her painting would reinforce the culture of belonging we are inculcating at Arrupe.

"Also," Janet wrote, "I will depict them with closed eyes and deeply within themselves conveying the private individual journey we all share and a longing for closeness to God. The central figure," she continued, "will be a young Latino Jesus Christ of the same age as the others and presented with a halo. Jesus will be the binding force of this painting, unifying all, and will hold his hands out in offering as will other subjects. This invitational gesture is meant to convey welcome to the viewer—to Jesus and to Arrupe College and education." Reading Janet's words was like praying. It was also an answer to a prayer.

The agreement between Janet and Arrupe College was reached in March 2016. In July, Wendolyn announced that a package had arrived in my name. Inside was the 36″x48″ canvas painting. I couldn't wait to open it! I called Janet immediately. "The painting is out of this world," I exclaimed. "The postures of the figures really strike me—they are filled with great dignity." I gushed on, "I really admire our students at Arrupe College, and the figures of this painting help me to understand why I admire them—because of their dignity." I paused, and then said. "I'm thinking of calling the painting *Jesus of Arrupe College*. OK by you?"

Janet responded with her characteristic eloquence. "I am relieved and happy to know the painting speaks to you, and especially in the way that it does," she said. "Young people have a special place in my heart, and work, and I strive to depict them with strength, courage, presence, and, as you say, dignity." Our conversation concluded with her blessing of the title. "Yes," Janet said, "it is OK with me if you wish to call the painting *Jesus of Arrupe College,* for it really is that, isn't it? This work has been a labor of love, complicated and sincerely from the heart, and I hope and pray that your students will feel welcomed and affirmed." A labor of love, complicated, sincerely from the heart, where students feel welcomed and affirmed—Janet described in a nutshell the essence of our work here.

A month after its arrival *Jesus of Arrupe College* was unveiled—a block away from the college, at Chicago's Holy Name Cathedral. Arrupe students, faculty, staff, family, friends, and board members were gathering for a liturgy to celebrate the end of the summer enrichment program and the beginning of Arrupe's second academic year. Before mass, Wendolyn and Jennie's administrative assistant, Diana Sayago, along with a handful of students, took the canvas to the cathedral. Once there, we arranged for it to be displayed in the sanctuary. Incoming students, rising sophomores, and other members of the Arrupe community filed in and gazed at Janet's amazing work.

The painting was naturally the prop for my homily. The gospel was from Matthew, and I focused on the following verse: "'Look! The virgin will conceive and bear a son, and they will name him Emmanuel,' which means 'God with us'" (1:23). Janet's painting, I said, helped me to understand what Matthew wrote, and I conveyed my belief that God is very much with us at Arrupe College because God is so obviously working with and through our students."*Jesus of Arrupe College* is inspiring," I said. "And look around—our city's cathedral is chock-full of beautiful works of art."

I paused and looked at the students. Some were accompanied by their grandmothers; others were accompanied by their babies. Some were citizens; others were undocumented. Some lived with their families; others lived at Mercy Home. Some were on the dean's list; others struggled academically. "I have to say," I continued, "that the most beautiful works of art in this cathedral today are all of you—you and your talent and your goodness and your commitment and your desires help me understand what Matthew means when he writes that God is with us. God is with us because of you."

Headcount: August 29, 2016

When one loves, one does not calculate.
—Thérèse de Lisieux

At each Arrupe board meeting I review key metrics. For example, I might run through these numbers for Arrupe:

- female/male ratio: 59 percent/41 percent
- average ACT: 17.6
- average high school grade point average: 2.8

- students who self-identify as persons of color, 97 percent
- students who are below the poverty line, 90 percent
- students who qualified for free and reduced price meals at their high schools, more than 90 percent
- number of freshmen in the class of 2018: 187
- number of sophomores in the class of 2017: 131

The last metric is, I contend, our first key performance indicator, and the number I've been tracking since the day we began. One hundred fifty-nine young people enrolled in the class of 2017 and began classes with us as freshmen in August 2015. A year later, 131 of them are continuing on at Arrupe as sophomores.

Our freshmen/sophomore retention rate is 82 percent. Jennie Boyle found that the freshmen/sophomore retention rate for two-year colleges in the United States is 53 percent; in Illinois, it is 54 percent.

This may be an unfair comparison. Our students come to us immediately after graduating from high school, whereas the average age of a community college student is twenty-seven, and that student is likely to be balancing classwork with parenting and a job—although that is also true of more than a few Arrupe students. In addition, many community colleges enroll students with more financial resources than Arrupe students enjoy.

The freshmen/sophomore retention rate for the twenty-eight US Jesuit colleges and universities has been 85 percent for the past several years. Early on, I drew a line in the sand. "We are a Jesuit college," I said. "Let's shoot for a retention rate of 85 percent." Some friends rolled their eyes. Another unfair comparison, they said. The majority of freshmen enrolling at Loyola University Chicago and the other Jesuit post-secondary institutions have considerably higher ACT scores and GPAs than the ACTs and GPAs I report to the Arrupe board members.

At first, I was disappointed by the 82 percent. I was saddened, really, because the number represents students who began with us who are no longer enrolled. Malikah, arrested last fall. Dante, overwhelmed by the shooting of his best friend. Esther and Jessie, unable to navigate college while raising children. Dashaun, suffering from periods of homelessness. Vincent and Valerie, engaging in self-destructive behaviors that prevented them from being successful. I identify with the gospel story of the Good Shepherd, and the students on this roster feel a little bit like my lost sheep. Career coordinator Farrah Ellison-Moore worked with all of them to find jobs or other opportunities. I'm admittedly biased, but I believed Arrupe was the best opportunity for these young people.

Why not a higher retention rate? Perhaps our initial schedule of five eight-week sessions, with two classes each session, had been too much for some of our students. The focus on two classes was beneficial, although not a good preparation for successfully transitioning into four-year colleges or universities, where students generally enroll in four or five or more classes per semester. Our classes met for three hours—a long time for many of our students. Eight-week sessions moved rapidly; by the time a student realized she was falling behind or he was struggling, there was little time to recover. We have since shifted to the traditional fall/spring semester model, with a summer session in order to work with our students year round. We believe that taking four classes during fifteen-week fall and spring semesters and two classes in nine-week summer sessions will benefit our students.

When I was lamenting our retention rate with a board member, he reminded me that our students had no precedents and suffered from lack of peer role models. There were no higher-level students to serve as orientation leaders, to offer their experience, and to serve as mentors. For our second year we could count on our sophomores to model for the new class what success and persistence mean at Arrupe.

Finally, there were plenty of other metrics that indicated obstacles for our students. Two had parents who were deported.

Three lost family members and close friends to gun violence. Four had babies during our first year. Five experienced homelessness. Over thirty struggled with immigration issues. Many experienced food insecurity. Many were affected by the spike in violence in Chicago.

I shared all of this with our board in an email. I also shared that our successes with our inaugural class resulted from the efforts of our generous, talented, and committed faculty and staff. I characterized our style at Arrupe as intrusive—we know a lot about our students, their backgrounds, their families, their strengths, their challenges, their aspirations because we spend time with them, we listen to them, we admire them. Our work at Arrupe is a combination of the *cura personalis* that has guided my ministry and the ministries of countless others in Jesuit works and following metrics—tracking attendance, drops in test scores, missing assignments—and being intrusive about the metrics.

"You are intrusive, I'll say that," responded board member Mark Shriver. "Seriously, congrats!"

"Congrats," echoed Preston Kendall. "This after just your first year of existence. It is really exceptional."

"This really is a testament to the faculty and the students who have the strong desire to learn and succeed despite all odds!" wrote Anita Alvarez. "*Adelante!*"

"Congratulations to you and your hard working team," responded Derrick Blakley. "It shows that higher expectations can produce higher results, if students are surrounded by proper supports."

Luis Gutierrez shared a quote from Thérèse de Lisieux: "When one loves, one does not calculate."

Susana Mendoza concluded the board's reactions with one word: "Amen!"

Conclusion

Holy Thursday and Easter Sunday

You guys know about vampires? . . . You know, vampires have no reflections in a mirror? And what I've always thought isn't that monsters don't have reflections in a mirror. It's that if you want to make a human being into a monster, deny them, at the cultural level, any reflection of themselves. And growing up, I felt like a monster in some ways. I didn't see myself reflected at all. I was like "Yo, is something wrong with me? That the whole society seems to think that people like me don't exist?" And part of what inspired me, was this deep desire that before I died, I would make a couple of mirrors. That I would make some mirrors so that kids like me might see themselves reflected back and might not feel so monstrous for it.

—Junot Díaz

On Holy Thursday, March 24, 2016, I visited Sean O'Brien's literature class. Sean and the students were reckoning with a collection of short stories by Junot Díaz called *Drown*. Later, when I saw one of our students, Gabriela, reading her copy of the book outside of class, we talked about Junot Díaz. I shared with her that I had enjoyed reading *The Brief Wondrous Life of Oscar Wao*, and his most recent book, *This Is How You Lose Her*. Gabriela told me that she loved *Drown* and wanted to read Díaz's other books. Sean has lit that spark. What Sean did in the class I attended was more than provide a spark, however; he provided our students with four statements that helped them (and me) to enter into Easter more fully.

First, Sean told the students that what they bring to the text is valuable. Second, he explained that a book or work of literature is meant to be completed by the reader. Third, he reminded them that literature should ask more questions than it provides answers. Fourth, he argued that when you finish reading a good work of literature, you should know how to live better.

Observing this class, it was wonderful to see the students engaging with Sean and the book, particularly two students, Jason and Raina. I was impressed with how well they have found their voices at Arrupe. As the class warmed up, I was happy to see that Sheryl and Alistair and Felipe also gained the confidence to share their insights. Sean's line, "What you bring to the text is valuable," is powerful for our students to hear. I imagine that, at least for some, they had not heard that in other classrooms or in other settings. They are hearing from a white instructor that what they bring to the text is valuable.

The same can be said of the reminder that every book or work of literature is meant to be completed by the reader. It tells these students that they are contributing to a work of literature, and that what they have to say, their perspective, their point of view, brings value and completeness to a work of literature. I see our students completing and contributing to the larger landscape of Jesuit education and adding value there.

That a work of literature should ask more questions than it gives answers certainly fit when Gabriela at one point said in class: "Now, I have a question for everyone. I want to figure out what this collection of stories means for us." Not only was Gabriela raising a question, but she was also building community by doing so.

Sean's fourth statement—when you finish a good work of literature, you should know how to live better—also resonates. I hope and pray that by the time our students finish Sean's class, and their other classes, and in fact their two years at Arrupe, they know how to live better. I hope they feel valued and know they are contributing. I hope they feel comfortable with their questions and know their questions are valuable and that they will live better. They will know somehow that part of living better is that they are academically more confident and accomplished, and that they've been successful, and that they can take these tools to the next best chapter of their lives.

Now what does this have to do with the Easter story? The people at my parish of Saints Faith, Hope, and Charity were probably wondering the same thing as I walked them through this in my Easter Sunday homily.

What you bring to the text is valuable. In the resurrection text Mary is the announcer. Mary is valued. Jesus values Mary and other women. Mary is from a culture that does not value women. I'm in a culture that does not value women. So Mary is the conveyer of the good news, of the greatest news. She is valued.

The book is to be completed by the reader. When you look at Peter and Mary and the Beloved Disciple at the resurrection, they have changed, just as we believe that this experience at Arrupe College is changing Raina and Jason and Sheryl and Alistair and Felipe and Gabriela. So in the Acts of the Apostles reading from Easter Sunday, Peter is now more courageous; he offers an admirable and concentrated summary of the Jesus story. But Peter also continues the story of Jesus; he is building on the story. Peter says to his readers in the Acts of the Apostles, and to all of us today, that the story continues to be told through witnesses. We are those witnesses now. The story of Jesus is not completed in the gospel. It is continued by the reader of the gospel, the listener to the gospel.

Literature should ask more questions than it provides answers. Just like Gabriela asked a question of her community at Arrupe, on that first Easter Sunday Mary and Peter and the Beloved Disciple comprehended what was going on slowly, gradually. They grappled with the reality of Jesus's resurrection, both in what it meant for him and what it implied for them. Gabriela's question, "What does this work of literature mean for us?" is similar, I think, to what Peter and Mary and the Beloved Disciple were beginning to grapple with.

When you finish reading a work of good literature you should know how to live better. Again, returning to the Acts of the Apostles, we find that Peter tells his listeners that he has become an apostle of forgiveness; we are to recognize that we are forgiven sinners and that we should be freely offering forgiveness. And finally, we are reminded that evil and death do not have the last word.

We know that the resurrection is beyond history. And we are changed because of the resurrection. We are changed partially because we know how valued we are and how valuable we are to our God, just as our students come to believe how valuable they and their perspectives are. Arrupe College is very much a story of change. The story that we are invited to enter is the same as that we entered during Holy Week, when we walked the way of Jesus's last day. Now we join Peter as witnesses and make the resurrection alive in our own contexts and communities. It's a story that leaves us with many questions, including some simply stated ones: How do we participate in this story? How do we witness the risen Jesus? How do we effect change?

Finally, when it comes to living better, Peter's prescription of mercy and forgiveness is not a bad start. Again, these are lessons that the students at Arrupe College teach all of us who work here. We are accompanying them. We aren't saving them. We aren't "fixing" them. We aren't rescuing them. We are accompanying them, and they are accompanying us to better lives. And to being valued. And valuing others. And to contributing to the stories of our lives, the stories of Jesuit higher education, and the story of the risen Jesus. And yes, it is an activity that raises many more questions for me.

When I listened to Raina and Jason, when Gabriela asked how we can build community, and when Sheryl and Alistair and

Felipe participated in class discussions as thoughtfully as they did on Holy Thursday, that Thursday became even holier. And Jesuit higher education becomes holier as well.